ANGER MANAGEMENT SKILLS

LIVE WITHOUT ANGER

THE AUTHOR

Dr. PS Bawa is a Senior Neurosurgeon (Brain and Spine Specialist) based in Delhi. He did his M.B.B.S in 1984 from Maulana Azad Medical College, Delhi and Post Graduation in Surgery (M.S) in 1988. He then completed his Super-specialization (M.Ch) in Neurosurgery from G.B. Pant Hospital, Delhi in 1993. Dr. Bawa further specialized in Spine and Rehabilitation from Princess Royal Spine Injuries Unit, Sheffield-one of the largest centres in the United Kingdom. He is one of the very few Neurosurgeons in Asia to have done specialization in such a challenging field.

Upon his return to India in 1996, he took over the reins of Chanan Devi Hospital as its Medical Advisor and Strategic Planner and converted it into one of the leading Super Specialty Teaching Hospitals of Delhi. During that period, he developed a passion for Neuro-Psychiatry and Behavioural Neurosciences, which helped him in developing innovative Finance and Management skills. He is a pioneer of Endoscopic (Keyhole) Spine Surgery in India, which has today revolutionized the treatment of Disc Prolapse / Sciatica.

He has been Chairman of many International Conferences and an active keynote speaker at various forums. In 2004, Dr. Bawa was honored with the prestigious "Delhi Ratna" (Jewel of Delhi) award by the All India Association of Intellectuals.

He is actively involved in many charitable causes and is on the Board of Directors of many companies and Editor of *Total Health* and *Medical Law Reporter* - India's first journal on Medical Law. He has frequently been invited for talk shows on TV, while his articles are regularly published in many periodicals and newspapers. He is on the Expert Panel of the Disciplinary Committee on Neurosurgery in Delhi Medical Council. A Scholar on Religion and Philosophy for over 30 years, Dr. Bawa has introduced the concept of 3P and LifeShastra (living modern day life based on timeless wisdom or Shastras). For *Details log on to* www.drpsbawa.com.

ANGER MANAGEMENT SKILLS

LIVE WITHOUT ANGER

DR. PS BAWA

SHIPRA

This book first published in 2015 entitled as 'Live Without Anger'. And is now being reproduced as 'Anger Management Skills – Live Without Anger'.

₹450; US$ 15
ISBN: 978-93-91978-49-5

2024

Anger Management Skills – Live Without Anger

Research, Compilation and Commentary by
Dr. PS Bawa

Published by:
SHIPRA PUBLICATIONS
LG 18-19, Pankaj Central Market,
I.P. Ext., Patparganj, Delhi 110092
91 11 22235152/ 6152; 9650028065
info@shiprapublication.com
www.shiprapublication.com

CONTENTS

Dedicated to my late father
Bawa Gurcharan Singh, Advocate

A Great Man

Song of Myself

These are really the thoughts of all men in all ages and lands,
they are not original with me,

If they are not yours as much as mine they are nothing,
or next to nothing,

If they are not the riddle and the untying of the riddle
they are nothing,

If they are not just as close as they are distant
they are nothing.

This is the grass that grows wherever the land is and
the water is,

This the common air that bathes the globe.

Walt Whitman 1882

LIFESHASTRA & 3P CONCEPT

No one can escape the ordeals of life and gamut of emotions it brings along. Be it love, hatred, greed, ambition, fear or lack of self-esteem, emotions often act as temptations and force us to commit mistakes. Countless wise men have fallen prey to these in the past and many will continue doing so. But it's essential to equip ourselves with knowledge so that such blunders are never repeated again.

Now this is where LifeShastra and the concept of 3Ps come into play. LifeShastra helps in leading a wholesome and healthy life through the timeless knowledge of Ancient Wisdom, and 3Ps — Physicality, Philosophy and Practicality — concept acts as a solution for various day to day problems

Physicality: "First we spend health to gain money and then we spend money to gain health." This quote stands so relevant, especially when many ailments today are a result of stressful and unorganized lifestyle. Total Health Programme, a Holistic regime helps attain a healthy body by drawing inspiration from the ancient medicinal systems and integrating it with modern science.

Philosophy: There is always a thought process behind every action and in order to seek guidance, we rely on the experience of various sources. Shastras are one such source that provides the necessary moral strength and philosophical wisdom to deal with uncertainties of life. The concept is relevant as it derives its inspiration from ancient philosophers, religions and various cultures.

Practicality: A man cannot lead a life without assuming harsh realities of the physical world. However, with sheer efforts, he can change and transcend his limitations. Problems cannot be merely prayed or wished away, they have to be tackled with all the available resources. As a result, teachings of various religions and ancient philosophies have been compiled so that they can be positively applied in daily life.

PREFACE

Many a time I have been asked this question: of all the subjects to write on why did you choose anger? The answer to this question is two-fold.

First, during my 30 years of clinical practice, I have observed that apart from the physical repercussions of an ailment itself, many patients as a consequence suffer from constant bouts of anxiety and stress, leading to anger. The anger could be because of the physical ailment or the tedious rounds of treatment that they are going through. Relatives who are witnessing the struggle of their loved ones or are shouldering the responsibility of the patient's illness often are as angry. The over–riding question in their mind is: Why Me?

Secondly, I have, over the years, observed an increasing tendency of people from all strata becoming increasingly angry and violent often over very trivial issues. In fact, I very came to realize that anger has great power: It can bring down anybody and shows no preference to education, wealth, status, race or gender! Highly educated people, very wealthy people were behaving in a most uncivilized manner when angry. This led me to realize that there is either something very seriously wrong with us as individuals or the society as a whole.

On further evaluations and also during my many interactions with people, I found that, firstly, most people don't like getting angry but end up losing their temper far too often. Secondly, there is this nagging feeling that is it them or other people in their lives who are creating situations that drive them mad i.e. in whom does the problem lie? Thirdly, for how long can this go on and fourthly, what is the solution?

During my research, I was surprised to find out that despite the fact that anger is such a common emotion, in fact a universal one, occurring multiple times daily, modern day science still does not

> Not only have the Shastras explained well the concept of anger in spiritual and philosophical manner, but have also provided practical solutions for the same. The teachings in them may appear remote in time, but they are not remote in thought.

have a uniformly acceptable definition for it, far less a standardized treatment.

Since anger is a severe disturbance in our consciousness, I turned to the timeless knowledge of Religion and Philosophy or *Shastras* as we call them in Sanskrit. The effort is aimed at providing perspective to this problem, thus guiding us to the solution because if you can't control your mind, there is no way you can control anger.

The basic essence of all religions as you will read further on is the same – the great dictum of Vedanta 'That Art Thou'. The concept of "That" here is, of course, *Atman* or the Spirit which is known in other religions *as Sanctus Spirit,* in Greek *pneuma, in* Arabic *ruh*, in Hebrew *ruah*, in Egyptian *Amon* and in Chinese *chi.* So at least where science has not been able to achieve consensus – religion has.

Not only they have very well explained the concept of anger on both spiritual and philosophical manner in their own way but have also provided practical solutions for the same. The teachings in them may appear remote in time but they are not remote in thought. They disclose the working of primal impulses of the human mind which is the same regardless of race, gender and geographical location.

Many a time people question about the relevance of ancient teachings in the modern day life and find them trivial, tedious and almost irrelevant. The answer to this is - Human nature has not changed much and the problems of human life have not been superseded by advancements in science. These ancient teachings had value and significance even at the time they were composed – that's why they were composed in the first place! And in today's world where there is violence, diminishing ethical standards, increasing indifference, air of general ferment, cultural crisis and spiritual agitation, there is all the more reason to relate to them bearing in mind the environment when they originated, and bridge the distances of time and so that we can take their most relevant and permanent essence. Please remember that centuries of thought lies behind these teachings and the past has to serve as an inspiration for the future. As Socrates puts it: 'Let us turn over together that wise men have left us, glad if in doing so we make friends with one another.'

Applied Philosophy or practical application of the wisdom provided by the *Shastras* is an essential component towards solving the issue of our emotional upheavals, including Anger. It is aptly said that - No man is an Island, thus we must apply this knowledge in our day-to-day interactions with others. Knowledge without application is a futile intellectual exercise. Thus many practical solutions from various religions, philosophers and even great generals and astute political advisors have been included from all across the world. Great Greek philosopher Aristotle very wisely answers when asked: 'What is the use of philosophic and practical wisdom?' To this he said: "Philosophic wisdom is the formal cause of happiness; practical wisdom is what ensures the taking of proper means to the proper ends desired by moral virtue."

Every person's journey, at the end of the day is that of self-discovery or an attempt towards it. We all witness innumerable human problems and sufferings, many of which are our own and thus LifeShastra (how to live life according to *Shastras*) has evolved in a bid to deliver ancient wisdom and knowledge from all over the world, from different cultures and times to as many people as possible in an effort to make a positive difference in their lives.

The book has been written in the format of 3P Concept: Physicality,

Philosophy and Practicality. I have tried to explain the mental and physical effects of anger, the essence of various religions and teachings of various philosophies behind it and lastly the practical solutions they offer.

Modern day science is making great advances in our understanding of the complex circuitry of brain, the role of genes and environment. Progress in neurochemistry, neurobiology, neuroimaging is unraveling many secrets which hopefully would lead to better diagnosis and treatment of mental ailments. I have tried to infuse all this with its theories and therapies. Studies clearly indicate that poor physical health is associated with increased mental health issues and these are among the most overlooked, despite their potential to compromise self-management and increase the risk for serious complications. Indeed the WHO motto on Health Action Plan 2013-2020 is: No Health Without Mental Health.

Dr. PS Bawa

Note

This is neither a religious book nor it is on or about religion. To follow religious teachings is entirely an individuals' choice, which cannot be enforced. In an attempt to present a holistic view on anger, I have tried to include the views of many great saints, seers, philosophers and even historic political advisors. But again for each there are many interpretations and how much one follows or agrees with them is left entirely to the reader. Though every attempt has been made to impart accurate information, this book serves only as a general guideline.

DEFINING AND UNDERSTANDING ANGER

Chapter 1

Every one of us, without an exception, has experienced a very strong emotion called anger—its fury and flames, its madness and infernal energy. Be it at our workplace or at home, with relatives or strangers: outbursts of anger in today's life can be triggered by trivial things such as a casual joke or while driving on the busy roads of our city. Anger has become so common nowadays that in many cases it is considered a person's Second Nature.

WHAT IS ANGER?

There is a confusion in both popular and professional literature regarding the definition of anger, which must be differentiated from irritation, hostility, aggression, and violence. We must begin with conceptual clarification of anger. Some define anger as a strong, uncomfortable emotional response to a provocation that is unwanted and incongruent with one's values, beliefs, or rights *(Thomas, 1995).*

Anger incidents are a common feature of everyday life *(Averill, 1982)* as individuals enact their social roles in families, schools, and workplaces. Unresolved angry confrontations with significant others can produce prolonged hurt and resentment. But anger is not synonymous with hostility, a chronic mistrustful negative attitude toward people and the world, or aggression, the actual or intended harming of another.

Aggression and violence can and do occur in cold-blooded fashion without anger *(Thomas, 1998).* And an expression of anger does not necessarily lead to aggression. In fact, it may even prevent aggression and elicit an apology from the other person *(Izard, 1993).*

Studies by research team *(Thomas, 1993; Thomas, McCoy, & Martin, 2000; Thomas, Smucker, & Droppleman, 1998)* as well as others *(Tice & Baumeister, 1993)* indicate that anger is an unpleasant, distressing emotion for most people, often mingled with anxiety and guilt. One study showed that people have fewer successful strategies for controlling anger than for any other emotional state (e.g. fear, anxiety, sadness, other strong feelings) *(Tice & Baumeister).*

Almost never do female study participants report that they feel good about the way they manage anger, whether they suppress it or vent it outwardly *(Thomas, 1993; Thomas et al, 1998).* Men and women both decry the failure of their anger outbursts in bringing about the desired responses from other people *(Thomas, McCoy, et al; Thomas, Smucker, et al).*

The adrenaline-caused arousal that occurs during anger lasts a very long time (many hours, sometimes days) and lowers our anger threshold, making it easier for us to get angry again later on.

The ability to handle anger effectively fits within the framework of "emotional intelligence", which has been defined as the capacity to perceive emotion, integrate it in thought, and understand and manage it *(Mayer, 1999).* Complete elimination of angry emotionality is difficult but not impossible but some say that anger has self-protective functions such as maintaining boundaries and mobilising courage to correct injustices.

There are a lot of synonyms like resentment, hostility, annoyance etc. to make it a socially acceptable term, but anger is best kept at bay not only because it leads to psychological changes in people, who fall prey to it, but also because it can severely affect a person emotionally and physically too. Some of us continue to be permanent victims of the tragedy brought about by it and are seeking ways to conquer it or at least diminish its intensity and frequency; however, not all those who have experienced anger are eager to overcome it. Many even rationalize their anger, and would go to any length to justify it, both to themselves and to others, as if the welfare of the world depended on their anger.

These days it is also intellectually fashionable to speak approvingly of the 'angry generation', as if anger, which is considered destructive at the individual level, when collectivized becomes a commendable virtue. Some people also seem to consider anger to be a kind of masculine virtue and wear it as a badge of leadership. Their philosophy can be put in a nutshell in these words: 'Rage supplies all with arms. When an angry man thirsts for blood, anything will serve him as a spear.'

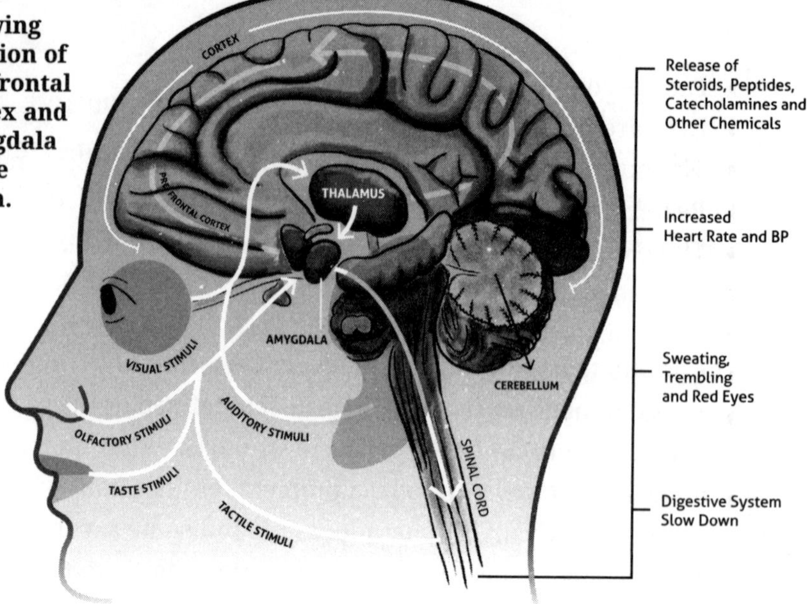

Showing location of Pre-frontal cortex and Amygdala in the Brain.

In advertisements, newspapers, electronic media, etc., we see anger and violence in great detail because it is happening all around us. Mental food of this kind can have a harmful effect on us. Yet, we wilfully seek this commodity and our voyeuristic pleasure in seeing rage and violence compels us like an addict to see more. It is necessary, therefore, to examine the phenomenon of anger both in its social and individual aspects, before devising strategies to overcome it.

PHYSIOLOGICAL REPERCUSSIONS OF ANGER: HOW IT AFFECTS YOUR BODY?

When one is angry, a variety of bodily changes occur, both external and internal. External bodily manifestations are obvious and observable. But the internal organic changes are detected only by special procedures, and modern recording devices including sophisticated diagnostic equipment. Following changes occur in the body at the time of anger:

- Face becomes red with excitement or anger;
- Eyes are protruded;
- The pupils of the eyes are dilated;
- Respiration becomes more rapid;
- The electrical resistance of the skin decreases;
- The blood clots more quickly at the time of injury;
- Blood sugar level increases to make the organism energetic;
- Gastrointestinal activities decrease or even stop totally;
- Blood is diverted from stomach and intestine to the motor organs and brain;
- The hairs stand on their roots.

All bodily changes during emotions are the result of a number of complex underlying processes originating in and integrated by the Autonomic Nervous System, the endocrine glands and the cerebrospinal system.

UNDERSTANDING PHYSIOLOGY OF ANGER

Emotions more or less begin inside two almond-shaped structures in our brains which are called the Amygdala. It is the part of the brain responsible for identifying threats to our well-being, and for sending out an alarm that results in us taking steps to protect ourselves. The Amygdala is so efficient at warning us about threats, that it gets us reacting before the Cortex (part of the brain responsible for thought and judgment) is able to check on the reasonableness of our reaction.

In other words, our brains are wired in such a way as to influence us to act before we can properly consider the consequences of our actions. People can and do control their aggressive impulses and you can, too, with some practice. This is the most important aspect which we have to understand.

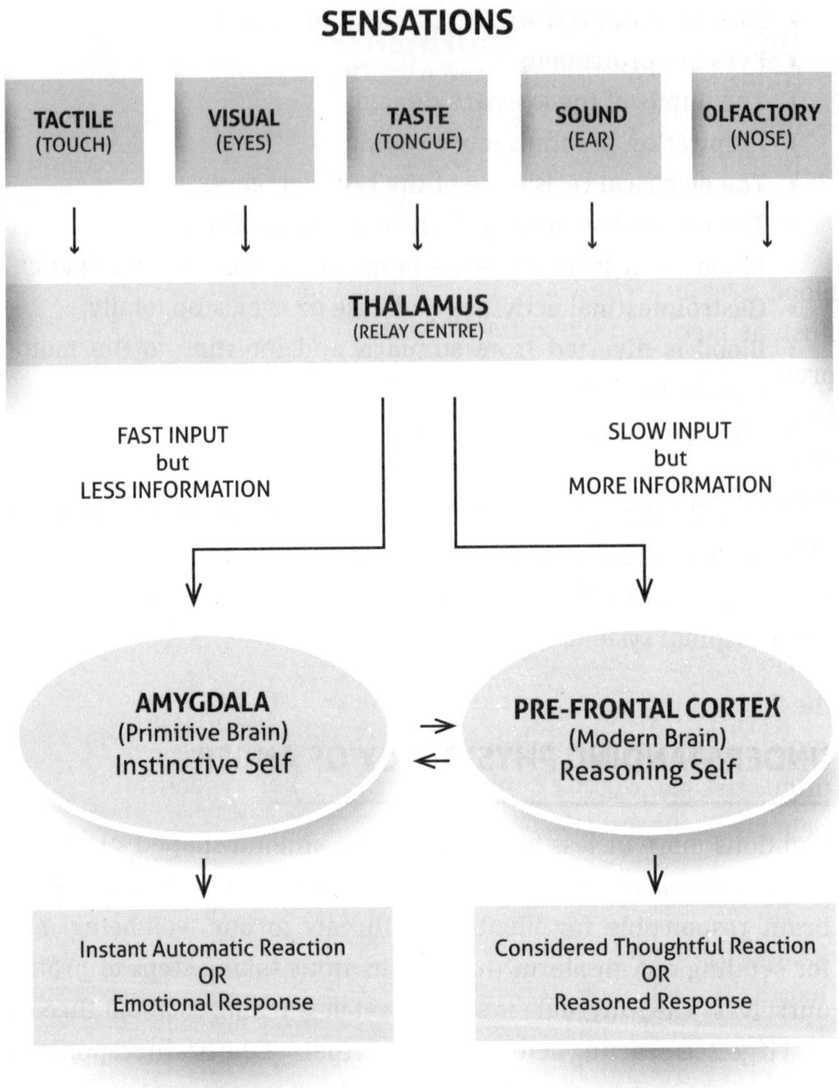

As one becomes angry, the body's muscles tense up. Inside the brain, neurotransmitter chemicals known as Catecholamines are released causing a burst of energy lasting up to several minutes. This burst of energy is behind the common angry desire to take immediate protective action. At the same time heart rate accelerates,

> The ability to handle anger effectively fits within the framework of "emotional intelligence", which has been defined as the capacity to perceive emotion, integrate it in thought, and understand and manage it.

blood pressure rises, and rate of breathing increases. Face may flush as increased blood flow enters the limbs and extremities in preparation for physical action. Attention narrows and becomes locked onto the target of anger. Soon one can pay attention to nothing else. In quick succession, additional brain neurotransmitters and hormones are released, which trigger a lasting state of arousal. Now one is ready to fight.

Although it is possible for emotions to rage out of control, the Pre-frontal Cortex of brain, which is located just behind the forehead, can keep emotions in proportion. If the Amygdala handles emotion, the Pre-frontal Cortex handles judgment. The Pre-frontal Cortex can switch off the emotions. It serves in an executive role to keep things under control. Getting control over anger means learning ways to help the Pre-frontal Cortex to get the upper hand over Amygdala, so that one has control over how to react to anger feelings.

Among the many ways to make this happen are the various techniques which reduce arousal, decrease Amygdala activity and help one practice using judgement to override emotional reactions. If anger has a physiological preparation phase during which resources are mobilized for a fight, it also has a wind-down phase as well. However, it is difficult to relax from an angry state. The adrenaline-caused arousal that occurs during anger lasts a very long time (many hours, sometimes days), and lowers our anger threshold, making it easier for us to get angry again later on. Though we do calm down, it takes a very long time for us to return to our resting state. During this slow cool-down period we are more likely to get very angry in response to minor irritations that normally would not bother us.

The same lingering arousal that keeps us primed for more anger also can interfere with our ability to clearly remember details of our angry outburst. Arousal is vital for efficient remembering. Moderate arousal levels help the brain to learn and enhance memory, concentration, and performance. There is an optimum level of arousal that benefits memory, however, and when arousal exceeds that optimum level, it makes it more difficult for new memories to be formed. High levels of arousal (such as are present when we are angry) significantly decrease your ability to concentrate. This is why it is difficult to remember details of really explosive arguments.

Research into aggressive behaviour has been divided into two types: Proactive and Reactive. Proactive aggressors plan how they're going to hurt and bully others, while reactive aggression, although, premeditated, occurs in response to an upsetting trigger from the environment. Reactively aggressive people — most commonly boys, frequently misinterpret their surroundings, feel threatened and act inappropriately aggressive. Their behaviour is emotionally 'hot', defensive, and impulsive. New studies from the University of California, San Diego are helping scientists better understand what goes on in the brains of some teenage boys who respond with excessive anger and aggression to perceived threats. Initial findings from these studies suggest that such behaviour is associated with a hyperactive response in the Amygdala, an area of the brain that processes information regarding threats and fear, and with a lessening of activity in the Frontal Lobe, a brain region linked to decision-making and impulse control.

In a related study, Frank and his colleagues are investigating whether these changes in brain activity are associated with an abnormal increase in hormones called Cortisol levels and decreased level of Serotonin, markers of the stress response. The brain chemical serotonin has long been known to play an important

High levels of arousal (such as are present when we are angry) significantly decrease your ability to concentrate. This is why it is difficult to remember details of really explosive arguments.

role in regulating anger and aggression. Low concentrations of serotonin in brain have even been cited as both a marker and predictor of aggressive behaviour. "Serotonin deficiency appears to be related to pathological, violent forms of aggressiveness, but not to the normal aggressive behaviour that animals and humans use to adapt to everyday survival," says Sietse de Boer, PhD, of the University of Groningen.

Furthermore, research now suggests that aggressive behaviour, if left unchecked, can eventually change the brain in ways that cause serotonin activity to decrease — and, perhaps, violent behaviour to increase.

More recently, de Boer and his colleagues have found that the transition from normal, adaptive aggressive behaviour into abnormal forms that inflict harm and injury is due to functional, but not structural, changes in certain serotonin receptors in the brain. In laboratory studies, treatment with selective serotonin receptor agonist, i.e. acting like compound has been found to restore the normal function of these receptors and suppress aggressive behaviour, including its escalated forms. These findings may one day lead to more effective treatments for violent behaviour in humans.

In scientific studies Corticosterone levels—a marker of stress, were found to be significantly increased soon after the end of the stressor session and those levels remained elevated for long periods. The increase was similar in both submissive and dominant subjects. Some cytokines also became elevated in the pre-frontal cortex of both groups of subjects, and this effect was greater after the stressful social encounters were repeated. In further studies, Audet observed that chronic exposure to social stress increased the sensitivity to a bacterial challenge and that this effect was more apparent in dominant subjects.

Being the recipient of an aggressive social encounter can cause changes not only in the brain that lead to depression, anxiety, but also increase susceptibility to immune-related illnesses, according to new studies from Carleton University in Ottawa. "It seems that aggression, which is clearly deleterious to the well-being of the victim, also has several negative repercussions for the aggressor as well," says Marie-Claude Audet, PhD.

Maternal Aggression: This form of aggression however is very different from the above and is related more to self preservation of species. Mothers are often at the receiving end of being over protective or even aggressive when it comes to their children. There is a biological reason behind this. Researchers have identified, for the first time, that the release of a neurotransmitter called arginine-vasopressin (AVP) in an area of the brain called the Amygdala helps regulate maternal aggression–a behaviour that ensures the survival of the offspring. Research into the neurobiology of maternal aggression has also found that Oxytocin, a neurotransmitter is released in the brain during birth and breastfeeding. Oxytocin reduces anxiety and fear, a factor that is believed to enable new mothers to more aggressively face intruders that might harm their offspring.

Social stressors and negative relationships are believed to contribute to stress-related disorders, including depression and anxiety. Stressful events have a profound influence on the neuroendocrine and neurochemical systems, causing chemical changes in many areas of the brain, including several that are strongly involved in emotions: the pre-frontal cortex, the hippocampus, and the Amygdala. Among the neurotransmitters and hormones altered by stress are dopamine, serotonin, noradrenalin, and Corticotropin-Releasing Hormone (CRH) (which affects blood levels of corticosteroids). Recent research has also suggested a link between stress and cytokines (signalling molecules within the immune system). Cytokines may inform the brain of the presence of pathogens in the body, thus triggering a stress-like response.

"Our findings suggest that stressful social experiences, by affecting central neurotransmitters and cytokines, may influence vulnerability to depression and susceptibility to immune-related illness," says Audet. He added, "Moreover, it appears that in addition to markedly affecting the victim's existence, aggression may have detrimental consequences also for the one that dominates the interaction."

The result simply put is this: Whether you are the one getting angry or someone is getting angry at you — both are equally harmed, the aggressor even more so. Anger not only affects you mentally, it also makes you weaker physically.

CONCLUSION

All scientific studies point that chemical transmitters in the brain regulate our response and reaction towards an external stimulus. The balance between them determines our perception, thought process, decision making ability and finally our response which may range from being a measured one to extreme socio-pathic aggression. These chemicals have been found to vary under different conditions, so can we modify and train ourselves to alter their levels in our brains? Science is now starting to explore the idea but religious philosophies certainly believe that it can be done.

HINDUISM ON ANGER

Chapter 2

In Hinduism, the essential qualities of a 'Hindu' are defined as 'those who uphold righteousness and fight ignobleness'. While Hinduism is based on the Eternal Truth, that is, to ultimately reach the abode of God, it is not written by one Seer or *Rishi*, but by many who relentlessly debated on and investigated into the facts, values and eternal truths of life, propagated not by a body of doctrines nor prophesied a controversial divine influence, but propounded by well-reasoned thoughts, codified in treatises and bequeathed finally to posterity. To put in other words, Hinduism is not based on the words of any single teacher or prophet, or on a single book.

INTRODUCTION TO HINDU LITERATURE

Hindu scriptures or literature have come to be so many in number and so comprehensive that there is more than one book in every branch of knowledge to suit and guide everyone, be he a beginner or a scholar or one in between.

The names of the *Shastras* or Scriptures that constitute 'Vedic Religion' or '*Sanatana Dharma*' are divided into two broad categories. These are **Sruthi** (Vedas, Upanishads, Upa-Vedas, Vedangas and Veda-upangas) and **Smrithi** (Ithihas, Puranas, Upa-Puranas, Smritis and Sutras.)

SRUTHI

'Sruthi' means that which is heard or acquired by hearing. They are regarded as Primary scripture. The eternal truths stated in 'Sruthi' had been revealed by God Himself; hence 'Sruthi' is considered divine in origin. The Truths emanated from God and God Himself communicated them to *Rishis* directly. It is the recorded knowledge in them that is heard or acquired and the same had been passed on by *Rishis* or highly evolved spiritual super-humans to their disciples or their grand disciples by word of mouth, the practice then prevalent. This had been done for centuries of generations. The contents of these literatures being what was heard originally by *Rishis* or acquired by hearing from them or from their disciples came to be called as 'Sruthi'.

SMRITHI

'Smrithi' means that which is remembered or written down from memory. They are the compositions of none other than *Rishis* who delineated, portrayed and illustrated in them the divine incarnations, Vedic *deva* or deities, *rishis*, etc. In these compositions, the *Rishis* incorporated the Truths and Principles mentioned in the Sruthi and described them through anecdotes, incidents and stories. Thus, in this way, Smrithi actually interpreted Sruthi texts in a practical way of life like their background and provided a human touch in their works. In fact, the personages involved in the interpretations or comments or teachings both Sruthi and Smrithi are no ordinary, but spiritual masters of very high order.

They are meant for reading and hearing. Actually they are intended for ordinary people or less intelligent people for meeting their devotional inclinations. These man-made literary works are considered as Secondary scriptures.

TEACHINGS OF BHAGAVAD GITA - SONG (GITA) OF THE GOD (BHAGAVAN)

Bhagavad Gita also called *Gitopanishad* contains divine words emanating from the lips of God Himself. Its glory is infinite, unlimited. None can really describe it.

As a scripture, the Gita embodies the supreme spiritual secret. It contains the essence of all the four Vedas. Its style is so simple and elegant that after a little study man can easily follow the structure of its words; but the thought behind those words is so deep and abstract that even a lifelong, constant study does not show one the end of it.

Upanishads, Brahma Sutra (Vedanta Sutra) and Bhagavad Gita are considered as the three top most foundational Vedic works on spiritual knowledge. However, it is the Bhagavad Gita, the song sung by God, that is considered supreme, because the God of it and in it is Lord Krishna, the complete eighth incarnation of Lord Maha Vishnu.

All the scriptures have originated from the Vedas. The Vedas were revealed through Brahma's mouths, and Brahma himself took his descent from the Lord's navel. In this way, a great distance separates the scriptures from the Lord. But the Gita has emanated directly

> The Vedas were revealed through Brahma's mouths, and Brahma himself took his descent from the Lord's navel. Gita has emanated directly from the lips of the Lord; hence there will be no exaggeration if it is declared as superior to all the scriptures. The Gita teaches not for renunciation of action but renunciation of inaction. It stresses upon carrying on our duties, effectively or ineffectively without attachment and the desire for the fruits thereof.

from the lips of the Lord; hence there will be no exaggeration if it is declared as superior to all the scriptures.

This Hindu scripture is a part of the Hindu epic Mahabharata which is set in a narrative framework of a dialogue between Pandava prince Arjuna and his guide and charioteer Krishna in the battle field of Kurukshetra.

Facing the duty to kill his relatives, Arjuna is counselled by Krishna to "fulfil his *Kshatriya* (warrior) duty as a warrior and kill."

Inserted in this appeal to *kshatriya dharma* (heroism) is between diverging attitudes concerning and methods toward the attainment of liberation (*moksha*).

The Mahabharata, the world's longest book is compared to a lamp and Gita a short chapter in it to the light in it. In Gita, the battle field at Kurukshetra represents tough situations of life within us where a struggle is waged by every one of us against negative, passive and evil inclinations. Many believe that this is why Lord Krishna chose the battlefield to give the sermon.

The Gita teaches not for renunciation of action but renunciation of inaction. It stresses upon carrying on our duties, effectively or ineffectively without attachment and the desire for the fruits thereof.

The Holy book stresses that the ego in man, looking for God should be cast away as a prerequisite. According to a man's level of comprehension, state of life, *ashram* and his mental suitability, he can choose any one of the paths or all or blended to realise God.

Sri Krishna refers to '*krodha*' or anger in many verses in the Gita. According to him, when a man dwells on objects, he feels an attachment for them. Attachment gives rise to desire, and desire breeds anger. From anger comes delusion; from delusion, failure of memory; from the failure of memory, the ruin of discrimination; and from the ruin of discrimination the man perishes. *(The Gita, 2: 62 and 63)*

Arjuna asked: O Sri Krishna! Under what compulsion does a man commit sin in spite of himself and driven, as it were, by force? *(The Gita, 3.36)*

Bhagavan said: It is desire; it is anger, which springs from Rajas. Know that this is our enemy here, all-devouring and the cause of all sin. *(The Gita, 3.37)*

Ostentation, arrogance, and self-conceit, anger as also harshness and ignorance —these belong to him who is born to the heritage of the demons. *(The Gita, 16:4)*

Possessed of egotism, power and pride and also of lust and anger, these people, envious by nature, hate Me in the bodies of others and in their own. *(The Gita, 16: 18)*

These three are the gateways of this hell leading to the ruin of the self — lust, anger and greed. Therefore let man renounce these three. *(The Gita, 16:21)*

Forsaking conceit and power, pride and lust, anger and

In the Gita, Sri Krishna utters in the same breath *Kama-Krodha-Lobha* — desire, anger and greed — as three gates to hell.

> *The Lord teaches:* First mark it out — anger is your prime enemy. Unless you name your enemy as your enemy, you can neither knock it out, nor have the will and enthusiasm for the battle.

possessions, tranquil in heart, and free from ego — he becomes worthy of being one with Brahman. *(The Gita, 8:53)*

In Sri Krishna's Teachings we have a complete system for overcoming anger, as it is based on a sound psychology and includes disciplines which all can practise whatever be one's religious denomination.

The Bhagvan says: Know that this is our enemy here, all-devouring and cause of all sin. *(The Gita, 3.37)*

One of the traits of delusion and ignorance is that we tend to take an enemy for a friend and a friend for an enemy. So, Sri Krishna instructs us to mark out anger as a direct enemy and treat it as such. Otherwise anger overcomes us with the aid of our willing and liberal help.

As we always get angry at any pretext, anger has become our friend by familiarity or association. Whenever we come under the power of anger we become deluded. Then we act like an ignorant person driven by *viparita bhav* or contrary understanding.

The words and actions prompted by anger are very forceful because those are directly connected with the source of energy within us, which is desire. We must remember that any source of energy embedded in the psycho-physical system of man is significant. Anger will have to be overcome in a manner that does not injure the energy resources. While the elemental force of fire is vital we cannot allow free movement of fire in our houses.

Overcoming anger will therefore mean separating the energy source in man from its destructive aspect, without destroying the power source itself. Every iota of power embedded in the system is needed for bringing about our self-transformation. In Hindu thought, emasculation is never considered to be an appropriate means to effect one's self-regeneration.

It is also noteworthy that in the Gita (16.21) Sri Krishna utters in the same breath *Kama-Krodha-Lobha* — desire, anger and greed — as three gates to hell.

These emotions are psychologically inter-linked, originating as they do from Rajas (action). Again the Bhagvan says: It is desire, it is anger, born of the energy or Rajas, all-devouring, all sinful, that you must know as your foe here. *(Gita: 3.37).*

Now having the vital knowledge about the origin, nature and destructive power of anger, and also by implication, the know-how of overcoming it, we should look into the following lessons:

- Anger, desire and greed lead to ruination.
- From anger comes delusion, from delusion comes failure of memory; from failure of memory, the ruin of discrimination and from the ruin of discrimination, man perishes.
- Anger is a quality of the demoniac part of human nature. Others negative and damaging emotions are display of wealth, arrogance, self-conceit, harshness, and ignorance; and they always move together and never in isolation. It is indeed a powerful gang. Therefore, in facing these brutes we must be more determined, courageous, innovative and skilful than the members of this gang put together. Though the job is not an easy one, the Lord gives us the assurance that anger can be overcome. And he also gives an important hint as to how this is to be done.
- The Lord teaches: First mark it out — anger is your prime enemy. Unless you name your enemy as your enemy, you can neither knock it out, nor have the will and enthusiasm for the battle. Our modern tendency is to temporize. He who does not call anger as man's enemy is sabotaging himself. Man is driven to commit many sins propelled by '*kama*' and '*krodha*', desire and anger.

So anger is not an innocent aberration, but the origin of a host of sins, and hence a foe.

- The Lord tells us how we can really measure up to this powerful enemy. He reassures us that anger originates from Rajas and has to be rooted out at that point of origin. By forsaking the evil passions one will become tranquil and thus be endowed with an inner atmosphere for a battle against Rajas in one's constitution.

THE BHAGAVAD GITA CONTAINS THE FOLLOWING TEACHINGS:

ON SELF HELP OR EFFORT

- Man must elevate himself by his own mind and should not degrade himself, for the mind is one's own friend and his own enemy as well. *(Gita: 6.5)*
- One who has steadfastness and sincerity can obtain wisdom. *(Gita: 4.39)*
- One who doubts will have neither this world not the world beyond nor any happiness. *(Gita: 4.40)*
- Without the observance of disciplines no good can be acquired. *(Gita: 6.55)*

ON NATURE BORN QUALITIES

- Nature born qualities of Sattva (goodness or purity), Rajas (passion) and Tamas (dullness or inertia) firmly ties the imperishable soul to the body. *(Gita: 4.5)*
- *Sattva* being immaculate binds through self-identification with happiness and wisdom. *(Gita: 14.6)*
- *Rajas* binds the soul through attachment to action and their fruits. *(Gita: 14.7)*
- *Tamas* binds the soul through error, sloth and sleep. *(Gita: 14.8)*
- Passion, anger and greed, these three constitute the triple gates to hell leading to damnation of the soul. Therefore, one should shake off all of these. *(Gita: 16.21)*

ON SENSES

- Senses are superior to the objects, the mind is superior to the senses, the intellect is superior to the mind and that which is superior to the intellect is He the Self. *(Gita: 3.42)*

ON MIND

- It is undoubtedly very difficult to control the restless mind, but it is possible by constant practice and by detachment. *(Gita: 6.35)*
- He whose senses are mastered has in his mind become stable. *(Gita: 2.61)*

ON SENSE OBJECTS

- The contact of the senses with their sense objects which give rise to the feeling of heat and cold, pleasure and pain etc, are transitory and fleeting, learn to bear them patiently. *(Gita: 2.14)*

ON WISE MAN

- The pleasures that are contact born are only sources of pain and such pleasures have a beginning and an end. It is for this reason that a wise man does not indulge in them. *(Gita: 5.22)*

ON MAN OF VIRTUE

- Fearlessness, absolute purity of heart, cultivation of mind in meditation for spiritual knowledge, charity, self-control, performance of sacrifice, study of Vedas, austerity and simplicity, non-violence in thought, word and deed, truthfulness and geniality of speech, absence of anger, renunciation, tranquillity of mind, abstaining from idle pursuits, sublimit, forgiveness, fortitude, cleanliness, absence of malice and absence of passion for honour, these are the marks of one who is naturally endowed with divine virtues. *(Gita: 16.1-3)*

ON MAN OF SPIRITUAL VIRTUE

- When a man abandons all desires of mind and is satisfied in the self by the self, he is said to be stable in wisdom. *(Gita: 2.55)*
- He is unshaken in adversity, completely unattached to pleasures and free from attachment, fear and anger. Such a person is indeed a sage of steady wisdom. *(Gita: 2.56)*
- He who is everywhere unattached, neither rejoices at the good nor is vexed by the evil, is a master of perfect wisdom. *(Gita: 2.57)*
- Absence of pride, freedom from hypocrisy, non-violence, forbearance, straightness of body, speech and mind, devout service of the preceptor, internal and external purity, steadfastness of mind and control of mind , body and senses. *(Gita:13.7)*

ESSENCE FROM DOCTRINES OF BHAGAVAD GITA

The grand edifice of the Ethics of the Bhagavad Gita has been built on the Eternal corner-stones of: (1) Immortality of the Soul; (2) Divine presence of God; (3) Constantly changing world: and (4) an Urgent Desire for Liberation. Because these truths are universal, the Ethics of the Bhagavad Gita also have universal application.

The revelation of the Immortality of the Soul in the *Sloka*:

'Ajo Nityah-sasvatoyam Purano Na Hanyate Hanyamane Sarire'. (Gita 2:20)

The soul is never born or dies; not does it become only after being born. For it is unborn, eternal, everlasting and ancient; even though the body is slain, the soul is not.

The Lord warns man not to deceive himself by trying to ignore the Law of *Karma*, the Law of Rebirth and the Law of Retribution.

The soul within him does not die with the death of the body; and, so long as it does not liberate itself by attaining *Jnana*, is bound to reap the harvest of the seeds it has sown in this birth-*Dhruvam Janma-Mritasya.*

The *Jiva* (living being) which imagines that it is the doer of an action is bound to it by an invisible thread called attachment. The action is a rubber ball with a long rubber band attached to it which is given to the children to play with; one end of the band is tied to the finger of the child and he throws the ball on the ground; and the ball promptly rebounds to the child's hand.

Similarly, every action performed by you with the idea that you are doing it, with a desire to attain a certain end, is bound to rebound on you sooner or later, in this birth or in another. Death itself is but going from one room to another; and so long as the band of attachment is not broken by the knife of non-attachment and the knot of desire born of ignorance is not loosened; the ball of action is bound to come back. One who realises this will do no evil. It is ignorance of the immortality of the soul and the inevitable working of the law of action and reaction that makes the wicked man go his evil way.

In the Bhagavad Gita, Lord Krishna explores righteousness. The greatest *Bhakta* is not the one who goes on rolling the breads, with selfishness, lust, anger and greed enshrined in his heart but the one who is endowed with all auspicious qualities, and who is devoted to the welfare of humanity.

> *Yoga, which rids one of woe , is accomplished only by whom who is regulated in diet and recreation, regulated in performing actions and regulated in sleep and wakefulness. (Gita 6:17)*

This *Sloka* aptly describes the Gita-ethics. The foolish extremes should be avoided; for they lead to the destination that is diametrically opposite to your goal. This is a simple but subtle truth which can be understood only by the diligent student of the Yoga of the Bhagavad Gita. To cite a simple instance, the man practising humility will go to the extreme of developing a pride in his own humility! The feeling that "I am humble" is as dangerous an obstacle as (if not more so than) the feeling "I am a powerful emperor"; the pride of erudition in the *Shastras* is as great an evil as pride in the knowledge of mundane sciences; and the man who rightly resolves to study the scriptures for his own enlightenment almost without his own knowledge slips into the extreme of intellectual dyspepsia which results in non-assimilation of the essence and vomiting of undigested material! Neither misuse nor disuse, but proper use is Gita Yoga. In fact the very word YOGA signifies this. It is the conjunction of two, the point at which the two opposites meet, it is the confluence of neither this nor that , but where both ends meet. The Lord has merely cited two examples of eating and sleeping and has commanded that you do not go to the extremes of fasting or indulgence, wakefulness or sloth. This principle should be applied to all the activities of man, to the entire life itself. This is the central teaching of the Bhagavad Gita.

> *Sri Krishna said: Arjuna, he who hates not light (which is borne of Sattva) and activity (which is born of Rajas) and even stupor (which is borne of Tamas), when prevalent, nor longs for them when they have ceased (Gita 14:22) and He who is ever established in the self, takes woe and joy alike, regards a clod of earth, a stone and a piece of gold as equal in value is possessed of wisdom, receives the pleasant as well as the unpleasant in the same spirit, and views censure and praise alike (Gita 14:23).*

These *Slokas* beautifully sum up the philosophy of the Middle Path. The sage standing on the firm rock of Self-Knowledge calmly lets the currents of Three *Gunas-Sattva, Rajas* and *Tamas* flow by, without courting one or running away from the other, that is to say when the body of the man who has risen above these Three *Gunas* is swayed by effects of *Tamoguna* in the shape of drowsiness, dream or deep slumber he feels no aversion for the same and when they relax their hold, he does not long for their return. Thus their appearance or disappearance makes no difference to him. He knows that in the All-pervading Light of *Satchidananda* (that alone is), the *Jiva* is a spark that flits about, changing apparent shapes, changing places and changing directions-now moving upward, now going forward and now diving downwards-but all the time in that Light of which it is an integral part and with which it soon becomes one. This understanding cautions you to avoid the twin-error of depending entirely upon self-effort or upon Divine Grace. The universe is maintained by the Divine Grace but the individual's self -effort is an integral part of the Divine Grace. The Lord declares: 'One is one's own enemy, and one is one's greatest benefactor. You will have to raise yourself by your own self". *(Gita 6:5)*

An ethically disciplined, morally purified and spiritually illumined soul is the goal of Gita-ethics. To attain this, the Lord exhorts the Man to spiritualise his entire personality. Of the three qualities that combine to make the personality of Man, *Sattva* is nearest perfection, *Rajas* is necessary evil and *Tamas* is inertia, lowest form of bestiality and waste of life itself. The aim of the Gita-ethics is to eradicate Tamas in Man, and by wise control of the *Rajasic* element to make it *Sattva*'s handmaid and to add to the quantum of *Sattva* in all possible ways.

THE THREE GUNAS

An entire chapter of the Gita is devoted to the classification of the major factors of man's life into the three qualities- *Sattva, Rajas* and

Tamas. Knowing this, man can avoid *Tamas*, keep the *Rajasic* to the minimum and strive in every way to grow more and more *Saatvic*. The following describe them in various aspects of life:

Worship: Worship of gods is good *Saatvic*. Worship of *Asuric* beings is *Rajasic*. Adoration of ghosts and evil spirits is *Tamasic*.

Food: Food which increases life, purity, strength, health, joy and cheerfulness, which are savoury and oleaginous, substantial and agreeable, is *Saatvic*. Food which is bitter, sour, saline, excessively hot, pungent, dry and burning is *Rajasic* food that causes pain, grief and disease. Stale, tasteless, putrid and rotten, refuse and impure is *Tamasic* food. Eat that food which will develop *Sattva* in you. Milk, butter, fresh ripe fruits, almonds, green dal, barley, parwal, torai, plantain, brinjal, etc, are *Saatvic*.

Yajna: Sacrifice offered by men, without desire for fruit, as enjoined by the scriptures, with a firm faith that such sacrifice is a duty is *Saatvic*. The sacrifice offered, seeking for reward, and for ostentation, is *Rajasic*. The sacrifice which is contrary to the scriptures, in which no food is distributed, which is devoid of *mantras* and gifts, and devoid of faith is *Tamasic*.

Austerities: The threefold austerity (of thought, word and speech) practised by steadfast men, with the utmost faith, desiring no reward, is called *Saatvic*. Austerity practised with the object of gaining honour and worship, by hypocrites, is *Rajasic*, and is bound to be unstable and transitory. That austerity which is practised out of a foolish notion, with self-torture, or for the purpose of destroying another, is *Tamasic*.

Charity: The charity given to one who does nothing in return, knowing it to be one's own duty to give in a proper place and at the proper time to a worthy person is *Saatvic*. The gift that is made with the expectation of a return or looking for some kind of reward, or made reluctantly is *Rajasic*. The gift which is made at a wrong –place and time, to unworthy persons, without respecting the receiver or insulting is *Tamasic*.

Renunciation: When a duty is performed merely because it ought to be done, without attachment or expectation of reward-the *Bhava* is one of *Saatvic Tyaga*. Renunciation of actions from fear of bodily trouble-because the action is painful-is *Rajasic* and does not bear the fruit of renunciation. Abandonment of obligatory action (which is not proper) on account of delusion is *Tamasic* renunciation.

Knowledge or Understanding: That by which one sees the One Indestructible Reality in all beings, the one homogeneous among the multifarious objects, that knowledge or understanding is *Saatvic*. That knowledge, which generates the perception of various entities of distinct kinds as different from one another, is *Rajasic*. But that understanding, which perverts the intellect and presents the unreal as the real, the part as the whole, is *Tamasic*.

Steadfastness (devotion): The unwavering firmness by which, through Yoga, the functions of the mind, the *Prana*, and the senses are restrained, is *Saatvic Dhriti*. The firmness by which, from attachment to fruits of actions, one holds fast to man does not abandon sleep, fear, grief, despair and also conceit is *Tamasic* firmness-it is foolish obstinacy.

Happiness: That which is like poison at first but is in the end like nectar, is *Saatvic* pleasure, born of the purity of one's own mind, due to Self-realisation. The pleasure that arises from the contact of the sense-organs with the object, at first like nectar, and in the end like poison, is *Rajasic*. That 'pleasure' which is at first and in the end sequel delusive of the Self, arising from the sleep indolence and heedlessness is *Tamasic*.

The world is as real as you are. As an individual you are a unit in this world. As Self you are the one with the world, one with the entire universe. On you depends the world and you depend on the world. There is not only mutual interdependence among the people in this world but also between people and celestials in the heaven - in other words between the whole universe. Therefore, Lord created *Yajna* - a spirit of self-sacrifice. This spirit of *Yajna*

> The world is as real as you are. As an individual you are a unit in this world. As Self you are the one with the world, one with the entire universe. On you depends the world and you depend on the world.

itself is the secret of Liberation. As a householder if you perform the following five great *Yajnas-Pancha Maha Yajnas*-daily with selfless service you will achieve Salvation. These include:

- ***Deva Yajna*** - offering sacrifices to gods which will satisfy the *devas.*
- ***Brahma Yajna or Rishi Yajana*** - teaching and reciting the scriptures which will satisfy *Brahman* and *Rishis.*
- ***Pitri-Yajna*** - offering libations of water to one's ancestors which will satisfy the *Pitris.*
- ***Nri Yajna*** - the feeding of the hungry and the guests.
- ***Bhuta-Yajna*** - the feeding of the animals.

YOGA SUTRAS: COMMENTARY BY SWAMI VIVEKANANDA

The word *Yoga,* is derived from the same Sanskrit root as the English 'yoke', meaning 'to join' that is - to join us to our reality, God. The *Yoga* disciplines of Patanjali are designed to lead an aspirant to Spiritual Liberation. The second *Sutra* of Yogasutras says: "*Yogaś citta Vritti nirodhah*". Anger is a modification of the mind, a *Chitta - Vritti.* Thus study of Yogasutras is essential to our understanding and conquest of anger. *Yoga* teachings cannot be applied. It has to grow out of you as flesh grows out of you and makes you what you are. The teachings must be assimilated so that it is no longer a foreign body, it has become you.

MODIFICATION OF THE MIND

The *Indriyas* (organs), together with the *Ahamkara* (mind), form the group called the *Antahkarana* (the internal instrument). They are but various processes in the mind-stuff, called *Chitta. Chitta* has been translated into 'mind stuff'- unconscious mind, conscious mind, super conscious mind, cosmic mind, individual mind and cosmic intelligence all put together. So *chitta* is the consciousness that is indivisible, undivided. It is the totality of the mind, the mind stuff, the totality of the intelligence which is indivisible, incapable of being partitioned-like space. The waves of thoughts in the *Chitta* are called *Vrittis* (literally 'whirlpool'). *Vrittis* are the apparent modifications of the mind-thoughts, emotions, feelings, memories etc. They are changing all the time. *Vrittis* are there not because you created them, but because the potentiality of *Vritti* formation is there in the mind. Right knowledge, wrong knowledge, imagination, sleep and memory are the five forms of the *Vritti* state within us, and all of them suffer from one universal characteristic- limitation. The word *Nirodhah* is very difficult to translate. It has been rendered into suppression or restraint. Therefore, the word 'understanding' explains it better than the words 'suppression' and 'restraint'. *Nirodhah* also means control, as in control of the car. Though it can be guided, attention can be focused. What is thought? Thought is a force, as is gravitation or repulsion. From the infinite storehouse of the force in nature, the instrument called *Chitta* takes hold of some, absorbs it and sends it out as thought. Force is supplied to us through food, and out of that food the body obtains the power of motion etc.

The real man is behind the mind; the mind is the instrument in his hands; it is his intelligence that is percolating through the mind. It is only when you stand behind the mind that it becomes intelligent. When man gives it up, it falls into pieces and is nothing. Thus you understand what is meant by *Chitta*. It is the mind stuff, and *Vrittis* that are the waves and ripples, rising in it when external causes impinge on it. These *Vrittis* are our universe.

We cannot see the bottom of a lake, because its surface is covered with ripples. It is only possible for us to catch a glimpse of the bottom, when the ripples have subsided, and the water is calm. If the water is muddy or is agitated all the time, the bottom will not be seen. If it is clear, and there are no waves, we shall see the bottom. The bottom of the lake is our own true self; the lake is the *Chitta* and the waves *Vrittis*.

The *Chitta* is always trying to get back to its natural pure state, but the organs draw it out. To restrain it, to check this outward tendency, and to start it on the return journey to the essence of intelligence is the first step in *Yoga*.

There is another class of *Vrittis* mentioned in the Ninth Verse of Yogasutra: *"sabda jnana nupati vastu-sunyo vikalpah"*or *Vikalpa* or imagination or verbal delusion from words having no corresponding reality. A word is uttered, and we do not wait to consider its meaning; we jump to a conclusion immediately. It is the sign of weakness of the *Chitta*. Now you can understand the theory of restraint. The weaker the man, the less he has restraint. Imagination is one of the favourite activities of the mind and leads to endless difficulties and problems.

Repetition of *Vrittis* of similar nature gradually builds up our *Samskaras* or nature, and again and again *Samskaras* in their turn give rise to similar thought-waves, the process working both ways. Here we come to grips with the problem of anger. Expose the mind to constant thought of anger and resentment and you will find that these *krodha-Vrittis* or thought-waves of anger, have almost unknowingly built up anger-*samskaras*, which will predispose you to find occasions of anger throughout your daily life. Those who are known to be bad-tempered, are the people who have gradually accumulated anger-*samskaras*. Such persons easily become victims of verbal delusion or *Vikalpa*.

If we can consciously remove the occasions of *Vikalpa* or verbal delusion from our interpersonal relations, occasions in which we have unpleasant or angry encounters will be sharply minimized. Anger has no definite and immutable cause. Anger has only adventitious pretexts for setting certain temperaments ablaze. The very same situation which will set a bad-tempered person red with rage, may only cause amusement to those who have not developed *krodha-samskaras*. Anger is not based on reason. Rather, a susceptible nature finds a reason for manifesting anger. So it is necessary to change one's character to be able to overcome anger.

A person's character is the sum total of *Samskaras*, acquired tendencies, which, however, is not impervious to change. As a sandbank of a river, looking sufficiently stable may change, when the currents of water change and flow in another direction, a character may change when the *Vrittis* change.

INSTRUMENTS OF KNOWLEDGE

We find in all beings three sorts of instruments of knowledge. The first is instinct, which you find most highly developed in animals; this is however, the lowest instrument of knowledge. What is the second instrument of knowledge? Reasoning. You find that most highly developed in man.

Reason can only go a little way and then it stops, it cannot go any further; and if you try to push it, the result is helpless confusion, reason itself becomes unreasonable. Logic becomes argument in a circle. Therefore there must be some other instrument to take us beyond, and that instrument is called inspiration. So instinct,

> Right knowledge, wrong knowledge, imagination, sleep and memory are the five forms of the *Vritti* state within us, and all of them suffer from one universal characteristic- limitation.

reason, and inspiration are the three instruments of knowledge. Instinct belongs to animals, reason to man and inspiration to God-men. But in all human beings are to be found, in a more or less developed condition, the germs of all these three instruments of knowledge. To have these mental instruments evolved, the germs must be there. And it must also be remembered that one instrument is a development of the other, and therefore does not contradict it.

FORMS OF YOGA

Yoga is the science by which we stop *Chitta* from assuming, or becoming transformed into, several faculties. As the reflection of the moon on the sea is broken or blurred by the waves, so is the reflection of the *Atman*, the true Self, broken by the mental waves. Only when the sea is stilled to mirror-like calmness, can the reflection of the moon be seen, and only when the 'mind stuff', the *Chitta* is controlled to absolute calmness, is the Self to be recognised.

There are various *Yogas*, or methods of unions- but the chief ones are-*Karma Yoga, Bhakti Yoga, Raja Yoga* and *Jnana Yoga.*

All the four *Yogas* are classified as following:

- ***Karma Yoga:*** The manner in which a man realises his own divinity through work and duty.
- ***Bhakti Yoga:*** The realisation of the divinity through devotion to, and love of, a Personal God.
- ***Raja Yoga:*** The realisation of the divinity through the control of mind.
- ***Jnana Yoga:*** The realisation of the man's own divinity through knowledge.

KARMA YOGA

Karma Yogi is the man who understands that the highest ideal is non-resistance, and who also knows that this non-resistance is the highest manifestation of power in actual possession, and also what is called the resisting of evil is but a step of the way towards the manifestation of this highest power, namely, non- resistance. Before reaching the highest ideal, man's duty is to resist evil; let him work, let him fight, let him strike straight from the shoulder. Then only, when he has gained the power to resist, will non-resistance be a virtue.

BHAKTI YOGA

Bhakti Yoga is the genuine search for the Lord - a search beginning, continuing and ending in love. According to Narada, *Bhakti* is intense love of God. When a man gets it, he loves all, hates none; he becomes satisfied forever. This love cannot be reduced to any earthly benefit, because so long as worldly desires last that kind of love does not come. *Bhakti* is greater than *Karma*, greater than *Yoga*, because these are intended for an object in view while *Bhakti* is its own fruition, its own means and its own end. A *Bhakt* passes through various stages to reach the Ultimate or *Para-Bhakti*. The preparatory phase is *Gauni*. The lowest form is *Shanta* or peaceful *Bhakti*. Next are *Dasya* or servantship, *Sakhya* or friendship, *Vatsalya* or loving God like a child culminating finally into *Para* or Supreme *Bhakti*.

JNANA YOGA

Jnana Yoga is divided into three parts. First: hearing the truth-that the *Atman* is the only reality and that everything else is *Maya* (relativity); Second: reasoning upon this philosophy from all points of view; Third: giving up all future argumentation and realising the truth. This realisation comes from (1) being certain that *Brahma* is real and everything else is unreal; (2) giving up all desire of enjoyment; (3) controlling the senses and mind; and (4) intense desire to be free.

Meditating on this reality and reminding the soul of its real nature are the only ways in this *Yoga.* It is the highest, but most difficult. Many people get an intellectual grasp of it, but very few attain realisation.

RAJA YOGA

Raja Yoga is divided into eight steps. They are **Yama:** non-killing, truthfulness, non-stealing, continence and non-receiving of any gifts; **Niyama:** cleanliness, contentment, austerity, study and self-surrender to God; **Asana**, or posture; **Pranayama**, or control of Prana; **Pratyahara**, or restraint of the senses from their objects; **Dharana**, or fixing the mind on a spot; **Dhyana**, or meditation; and finally **Samadhi**, or super-consciousness. The *Yama* and *Niyama*, as we see, are moral training; without these as the basis no practice of *Yoga* will succeed. As these two become established, the Yogi will begin to realise the fruits of his practice; without these it will never bear fruit. A *Yogi* must not think of injuring anyone, by thought, word, or deed. Mercy shall not be on men alone, but shall go beyond, and embrace the whole world.

Swami Vivekananda teaches in the *Raja-Yoga*: 'The *Chitta-Vrittis*, the thought-waves, which being gross, we can appreciate and feel; they can be more easily controlled, but what about the finer instincts? How can they be controlled? When I am angry, my whole mind becomes a huge wave of anger. I feel it, see it, handle it, can easily manipulate it, can fight with it; but I cannot succeed perfectly in the fight until I can get down to its causes'.

'When a man first began to abuse me, I thought, "I am going to be angry." Anger was one thing, I was another; but when I became angry, I was anger itself. These feelings have to be controlled in the germ, the root, in the fine forms, before we become conscious that they are acting on us. With the vast majority of mankind they emerge from the subconscious. When a bubble rises from the bottom of the lake, we do not see it, nor even when it has nearly come to the

> It is said, "Habit is the second nature," it is the first nature also, and the whole nature of man, everything that we are, is the result of habit. That gives us consolation, because, if it is only habit, we can make and unmake it at any time.

surface; it is only when it bursts and makes a ripple that we know it is there. We shall only be successful in grappling with the waves when we can get hold of them in their fine causes, and until we get hold of them and subdue them before they become gross'.

Swami Vivekananda explains: 'Each action is like the pulsation quivering over the surface of the lake. The vibrations die out but what is left? The *Samskaras*, the impressions. When a large number of these *Samskaras* are left in the mind, they coalesce and become a habit. It is said, "Habit is the second nature," it is the first nature also, and the whole nature of man, everything that we are, is the result of habit. That gives us consolation, because, if it is only habit, we can make and unmake it at any time. The *Samskaras* are left by these vibrations passing out of our mind, each of them leaving its mark. Our character is the sum total of these marks, and accordingly as some particular wave prevails one takes that tone. If good prevails, one becomes good; if wickedness, one becomes wicked; if joyfulness one becomes happy. The only remedy for bad habits is counter habits; all the bad habits that have left their impressions are to be controlled by good habits. Go on doing good, thinking holy thoughts continuously; that is the only way to suppress base impressions. Never call anyone hopeless, because he only represents a character, a bundle of habits, which can be checked by new and better ones. Character is repeated habits, and repeated habits can alone change character'.

FOLLOWING ASPECTS MUST BE KEPT IN MIND BEFORE TRYING TO OVERCOME ANGER.

- Patanjali's teachings firmly bear out the conviction that anger can be completely overcome. Anyone determined to do so, can achieve it, provided he has the required patience for practising the necessary disciplines.
- For overcoming anger, the phenomenon has to be clearly understood at the outset.
- Anger may be manifested variously. But anger cannot be overcome by handling manifestations in a piecemeal fashion.
- Anger at its root or origin is a *Chitta-Vritti*, thought-wave, a modification of the mind. For overcoming anger, these modifications of the mind need to be handled.

Patanjali teaches how the fine *samskaras* are to be controlled: 'These fine *samskaras* are to be conquered by resolving them into their causal state'. *(Yoga Sutras, 11.10).*

Swamiji explains this aphorism: '*Samskaras* are the subtle impressions that manifest themselves into gross forms later on. How are these fine *samskaras* to be controlled? By resolving the effect into its cause. When the *Chitta*, which is the effect, is resolved into its cause, *Asmita*, or Egoism, only then, the fine impressions die along with it. Modification cannot destroy this'.

In its origin anger is a thought-wave, or still earlier, a thought-bubble. This thought-bubble originates in *Avidya*, ignorance. Patanjali teaches: 'Ignorance is taking the non-eternal, the impure, the painful, and the not-self for eternal, the pure, the happy, and the *Atman* or the self (respectively)'. (II.5)

The internal organ or mind has four aspects. First-*Manas*, the cogitating or thinking faculty, which is usually almost entirely wasted, because mostly it is left uncontrolled; but when properly governed, it is a wonderful power. Second- *Buddhi*, the will (sometimes called the intellect). Third-*Ahamkara*, the self-conscious egotism (from *Aham*). Fourth-*Chitta*, the substance in and through which all the faculties act, the floor of the mind as it were; or the sea in which the various faculties are waves.

In the *Katha Upanishad* the body is described as the chariot, mind is the reigns, intellect is the charioteer, senses are the horses, and objects of the senses their road. The self is the rider, seated in the chariot.

This *Avidya* is invariably associated with *Asmita, Raga, Dvesha* and *Abhinivesha* — these are all obstructions to *Yoga*, and each of these make substantial contribution to *krodha* or anger. We need to understand these four companions of Av*idya*, which originate and rest in ignorance. *Asmita* that is egoism is the identification of the seer (*Atman*) with the instruments of seeing (mind and the senses). *Raga* is attachment to that which gives pleasure. *Dvesha* is aversion to that which gives displeasure or pain. *Abhinivesha* is clinging to life; anything obstructing that clinging causes anger. When we live a life of such a pattern, which is gross and worldly, *Avidya* and its harmful associates get more firmly entrenched. Then we cannot overcome anger and we become slaves of anger. But, it is possible and open to everyone of us to practise *Viveka*, discrimination, through which the effect of all these can be attenuated and eventually even *Avidya* can be destroyed by the grace of God. Those who want to overcome anger along with the practice of discrimination intended for attenuating the forces of *Avidya, Asmita, Raga, Dvesha* and *Abhinivesha*, must follow the precept that they should not allow their passions to linger in their minds.

EMBRACING POSITIVITY

Do not look on the fault of others. You cannot judge a man by his faults. (Example: Suppose we were to judge an apple tree by the rotten, unripe, unformed apples we find on the ground.) Remember, the wicked are always the same all over the world. It is only in the good and the pure and the strong that you find variety. Do not recognise wickedness in others. Wickedness is ignorance, weakness. What is the good of telling people they are weak?

Criticism and destruction are of no avail. We must give them something higher; tell them of their own glorious nature, their birth right. Why do not more people come to God? The reason is that so few people have any enjoyments outside their five senses.

ROAD TO SUCCESS

There are three things necessary for a student to succeed in life. These are:

First is to give up all ideas of enjoyment in this world and the next, care only for God and Truth. He must not spend himself in vain talking that bears no fruit.

Second is intense desire to know Truth and God. Be eager for them, long for them, as a drowning man longs for breath. Turn from all and seek only God.

Third is to follow six training procedures. These include:

- Restraining the mind from going outward
- Restraining the senses
- Turning the mind inward
- Suffering everything without murmuring
- Fastening the mind to one idea. Take the subject before you and think it out; never leave it. Do not count time.
- Think constantly of your real nature. Get rid of superstition. Do not hypnotise yourself into a belief in your own inferiority. Day and night tell yourself what you really are, until you realise (actually realise) your oneness with God.

The Yogasutra 1:33 says: *Maitri karuna mudito peksanam sukha duhkha punya punya visayanambha vanatas citta prasadanam.*

The following fourfolds attitude to life's vicissitudes and in all relationships, being conducive to peace of mind, enables one to overcome the distractions of the mind.

This is a very important Sutra beacause we are living in this world and it is full of these four types of people.

- Friendliness *(Maitri)* towards pleasure or those who are pleasantly disposed to oneself (friends).
- Compassion *(Karuna)* for the sorrowful and, when one is in a painful condition, self-forgetful sympathy for those who may be in a similar painful condition.
- Rejoicing *(Mudita)* in the exaltation of the exaltation of the noble or the holy ones, and
- Indifference *(Upeksa)* to unholiness, not being drawn into it nor holding others in contempt for their unholiness.

Ignorance, fickleness, jealousy, laziness and excessive attachment are the great enemies to success in *Yoga* practice. The Three (3P) great requirements are as follows:

- **Purity** both physical and mental: All uncleanness, all that would draw the mind down, must be abandoned.
- **Patience**: At first there will be wonderful manifestations, but they will all cease. This is the hardest period, but hold past; in the end the gain is sure if you have patience.
- **Perseverance**: Persevere through thick and thin, through health and sickness, never miss a day in practice.

SWAMI SIVANANDA'S COMMENTARY ON ANGER

According to the great religious scholar Swami Sivananda - Anger is a negative *Vritti* or whirlpool in the mind-lake; born of ignorance. It is a strong emotion, excited by a real or fancied injury; involving a desire for retaliation.

He stresses that anger is the natural passion or emotion of

displeasure and antagonism aroused by injury or insult, real or imagined, and directed against the cause thereof. Anger arises from an idea of evil having been inflicted or threatened. Anger is born of ignorance. Anger is a modification of desire. Anger arises from avarice, selfishness. Anger arises when one is insulted, abused, criticised or when his defects are pointed out.

Anger springs when a desire is not gratified. Anger comes when someone stands in the way of gratifying one's desire.

Anger manifests from loving one's own opinion; from desire of being honoured; from imagining that, one is wiser and superior than everybody.

Anger obstructs reason. Anger clouds understanding and poisons the blood, nerves and the whole system.

Anger is often accompanied by a desire to take vengeance, or to obtain satisfaction from the offending party.

It begins in folly and ends in repentance. When anger arises, one should always think of the consequences. Soon it will subside.

To become angry over trifling things is mean, childish and brutal. "Anger is personal and usually selfish, aroused by real or supposed wrong to oneself. Indignation is impersonal and unselfish displeasure at unworthy acts. Pure indignation is not followed by regret and needs no repentance. It is also more self-controlled than anger."

Anger is commonly a sin and it can be further classified into various types: Indignation is often a duty. We speak of 'righteous' indignation. Rage drives one beyond the bounds of prudence or discretion. Fury is stronger and sweeps one away into uncontrollable violence. Wrath is deep and vengeful displeasure. It simply expresses the culmination of righteous indignation without malice in a pure being.

Anger is manifestation of *Sakti* or *Devi*.

In "*Chandipath*" or "*Durga Sapta-Sati*" you will find:

Ya Devi sarvabhuteshu krodharupena samsthita,
namastasyai namastasyai namastasyai namo namah.

"I bow again and again to that Devi who is seated in all beings in the form of anger."

Anger resides in the *Linga Sarira* (astral body), but it percolates into the physical body just as water percolates through the pores to the outer surface of an earthen pot. Just as heat melts lead, just as heat and borax melt gold, *Kama* and *Krodha*, the heating factors of the mind, melt the mind.

Anger begets eight kinds of vices. All evil qualities and actions proceed from anger. If you can eradicate anger, all bad qualities will die their natural death.

These eight vices are: (1) Injustice, (2) Rashness, (3) Persecution, (4) Jealousy, (5) Taking possession of others' property, (6) Killing, (7) Harsh words, and (8) Cruelty.

When a man's desire is not gratified and when someone stands in the way of its fulfilment, man becomes angry. The desire gets transformed into anger. When one is under the sway of anger, he will commit all sorts of sinful deeds. He will lose his memory, his sense of judgement will become clouded and his intellect will get perverted.

Krodhat bhavati sammohah sammohat smriti-vibhramah:
Smritibhramsat buddhinaso buddhinasat pranasyati.

"From anger comes delusion, from delusion, loss of memory; from loss of memory, destruction of discrimination; from destruction of discrimination he perishes."

Anger is the greatest enemy. Contentment is the *Nandana* Kanan (the heavenly flower garden of Indra) and peace is the Kamadhenu. Therefore, take to forgiveness. *Atman* is different from the body, the *Indriyas, Prana* and the intellect. It is self-effulgent, unchangeable, pure and formless.

An angry man has the capability to commit murder. He himself does not know what he is exactly doing. He becomes emotional and impulsive. A man, when angry, will speak ill, do as he desires. A hot word results in fighting and stabbing. It's like he is intoxicated. He loses his consciousness and falls prey to anger.

Irritation, frowning, resentment, indignation, rage, fury, wrath are all varieties of anger. If a man wants to correct another man and manifest slight anger, unselfishly, as a force to check and improve him, then it is called "righteous indignation" or "spiritual anger". Jealousy is hatred. Anger is hatred. *Ghrina* is hatred. *Irshya* is hatred. *Asuya* is hatred. *Amarsha* is hatred. Remove hatred through love, prayer, *japa,* service and meditation. Anger acts as a boomerang because it injures the man who becomes angry. It comes back to the angry man and does harm to him. Therefore, control anger by *Kshama,* love, enquiry and service.

Self-restraint is a sign of great mental strength. An easily irritable man is always unjust. He is swayed by impulses and emotions. Anger gains strength by repetition. If checked immediately, man gains immense strength of will. When anger is controlled, it becomes transmuted into spiritual energy that can move the three worlds.

Just like heat or light is converted into electricity, similarly anger converts into *Ojas*. Energy takes another form. Energy is wasted enormously when one gets angry. Moreover, the entire nervous system gets shattered by an outburst of anger. The eyes become red, the body quivers, while legs and hands tremble. No one can check an angry man. He gets enormous strength for a brief period of time, but collapses after sometime on account of reaction.

Passion serves as the root and anger as the stem of this malady,

> Anger begets eight kinds of vices. If you can eradicate anger, all bad qualities will die their natural death. These eight vices are: Injustice, Rashness, Persecution, Jealousy, Taking possession of others' property, Killing, Harsh words and Cruelty.

therefore, it is important to destroy the root (passion) first and then the stem (anger) will die its natural death. The root cause of anger is ignorance and egoism. Through *Vichara* (right enquiry), egoism should be removed. Then alone can one control his anger completely. Through development of the opposite virtues such as *Kshama*, love, *Santi*, *Karuna*, friendship, etc., anger can be controlled to an enormous degree. The force can be reduced. *Atma-jnana* alone can try all *Samskaras* of anger and eradicate it too.

If an aspirant has controlled anger, half of his *Sadhana* is over. It's very difficult to say when a man will be thrown into a fit of fury. Therefore, anger should be controlled even when it is in the form of a small ripple in the subconscious mind (*Chitta*). One should watch his mind very, very cautiously.

Annihilate anger through love, forgiveness, enquiry, devotion, discrimination, wisdom, prayer, service, *Saatvic* food, selflessness, desirelessness, *japa*, meditation, *Nitya-Drishti*, *Dosha-Drishti* and *Tanmaya-Drishti*.

CONQUERING THE MIND

Mind is a bundle of *Vasanas* (desires) and *Sankalpas* (thought, imagination). Mind is a bundle of *Raga-Dvesha* (likes and dislikes). Annihilation of mind is *Manonasa*.

Manolaya is temporary absorption of the mind. This cannot give

> Passion serves as the root and anger as the stem of this malady, therefore, it is important to destroy the root (passion) first and then the stem (anger) will die its natural death. The root cause of anger is ignorance and egoism.

Moksha. The mind can come back again and wander in sensual objects. *Manonasa* alone can give release or *Moksha*.

However, those who seek to overcome anger must be sure that:

- Anger is destructive of everything they seek to achieve in life, worldly or spiritual.
- Anger, which has been called temporary madness, if not overcome, can become permanent insanity. Its fire can reduce everything to ashes.
- It is possible to overcome anger, though not very easily. This can be done through methodical, sustained self-effort and grace, say of God, or of one's own mind and efforts along with help of others.
- Self-effort is needed to overcome one's anger. This cannot be accomplished vicariously.
- In order to overcome anger we should have to change our very personality, by re-structuring or reorganizing our given nature.
- In the disciplines of *Yoga*, overcoming anger has to happen as a matter of course. It is done somewhere on the way, without giving special attention to it.
- Those who regard the attainment of spiritual illumination as their ultimate goal in life may be more forcefully motivated to overcome anger. However, it is not that a non-believer or cynic cannot overcome anger. He certainly can, provided he practises the same disciplines. He may not believe in God, but he must believe in spiritual values.

How is the mind purified, brought under control and how are its activities stopped, and how is it annihilated? Here are some useful and practical points.

BY *VICHARA*

Mind can be controlled and annihilated by *Vichara* or enquiry of 'WHO AM I?' This is the best and most effective method. This will annihilate the mind. This is the Vedantic Method. Realise the unreality of the mind through philosophical thinking.

BY ERADICATION OF EGO

Eradicate the feeling of egotism. Ego is the seed of the tree of mind. "I"-thought is the source of all thoughts. All thoughts are centered on the little "I". Find out what the little "I" is. This little "I" will dwindle into an airy nothing. It will be absorbed in the Infinite "I" or *Para Brahman*, the source of the little "I" or *Ahamkara* (egoism). The Sun of Self-realisation is fully seen when the cloud of ego disappears.

BY *VAIRAGYA*

Vairagya (dispassion) is another method of annihilating the mind. It is distaste of objects of sense-displeasures by finding out defects in the sensual life. Objects are perishable. Sensual pleasure is momentary and illusory.

BY *ABHYASA*

Abhyasa or practice is another method. Concentrate the mind by fixing it on *Brahman*. *Abhyasa* is ceaseless meditation. This leads to *Samadhi*.

BY NON-ATTACHMENT

Asanga or non-attachment is a sword to destroy the mind. Detach it from the objects and attach it to the Lord. Do this again and again.

The essence of the seed of the sprout of world experience, which is desire, can be destroyed by the fire of non-attachment.

BY *VASANAKSHAYA*

Vasanakshaya is another method. *Vasana* here means desire. Renunciation of desire leads to *Vasanakshaya,* which then leads to annihilation of the mind (*Manonasa*). Desire for objects of pleasure is bondage: giving it up is emancipation. Desire is the most essential nature of the mind. Mind and egoism are synonymous.

BY *PRANAYAMA*

Vibration of *Prana* causes movement of the mind. It gives life to the mind. *Pranayama* or control of *Prana* will stop the activities of the mind. But it cannot destroy the mind to its roots like *Vichara.*

BY CONTROL OF THOUGHTS

Control the thoughts or *Sankalpas*. Avoid imagination or day-dreaming. The mind will be annihilated. Extinction of *Sankalpas* alone is *Moksha.* The mind is destroyed when there is no imagination. The expriences of the world is an illusion due to your imagination. It vanishes away when imagination is completely stopped.

BY SELF-CONTROL AND BALANCE

Mental renunciation of possessions is another method. The absolute experience can also be released if you learn to be in a state of thought-suspending *Samadhi.* Attainment of self-control is another method. Be balanced in pain and pleasures, heat and cold, etc.

BY DEVOTION AND SERVICE

Japa, Kirtan, prayer, service of *Guru* and study are also means to annihilate the mind. He alone experiences everlasting peace and eternal bliss who has transcended the mind and rests in his own *Satchidananda Atman.*

IS THERE RIGHTEOUS ANGER?

Anger is very powerful; it can destroy all *Tapas*. It subdued Durvasa and conquered Yajnavalkya. It is the enemy of peace and the foe of knowledge. Born of *Rajo Guna*; it is all devouring. It is the gate of hell and destroys the Atomic Pearl. Anger makes the *Jiva* senseless and it makes him do all *Adharmas*. It makes him more furious by turning him into its slave, making him perfectly blind and losing his understanding. However, Hindu Mythology is replete with instances where Sages sometimes cursed for the violation of dharma which turned as a boon for the offender or else he would have to undergo repentance of a sinful act for several births. Sage Agastya cursed Kubera that his army along with Manimanta would be killed, as Manimanta had spit on Sage Agastya's head while he was performing morning prayers to Sun God. This punishment exculpated him from the sin. Sage Maitreya cursed Duryodhana that his thigh would be broken in the war as he was not attentive to his advice and was patting his thigh.

Maharsi Ved Vyasa gave a special rule of morality though anger was considered to be one of the ills to be avoided. In chapter 28 of *Vana Parva* it is said: "People should not be always angry or mild; they should exhibit their anger or mildness in proper hours." In the next chapter he also said: "Anger is the destroyer of mankind, and anger again places them in prosperity; anger is the root of prosperity and adversity." The secret of this rule is one should not succumb to anger but it must be used as an instrument. We got an excellent example in Ramayana as Sri Rama invites Krodha and *Rosa-Krodham Aharyamasa; Rosam Aharyamasa,* - i.e. he used to call 'anger' and 'wrath' whenever needed and after the use, he used to leave that anger or wrath as an instrument like a sword and a bow.

However, there are people who consider anger so useful that they refuse to learn how to overcome it. If we have not learnt how to overcome anger, we cannot use anger deliberately for any creative purpose. It is a difficult task to utilize anger masterfully and deliberately thus for a normal person it is best to eliminate it completely.

MEDITATION

Modern day science is now realizing what religion has said all along: that Meditation and reciting *Mantras* has immense influence on our Inner Self and its positive energy manifests itself both on our physical as well as our psychological well-being. To quote just two studies:

- Relationship of frequent *Mantra* repetition to emotional and spiritual well-being in Healthcare workers *(Becker S, Gershin M et al, Journal of Continuing Education in Nursing, 2006, 37(5): 218-224)*:

  Healthcare workers report high levels of stress in the workplace. To determine how to reduce stress, the authors examined the effectiveness of frequently repeating a *mantra* (a word with spiritual meaning) on emotional and spiritual well-being. A pretest-posttest design was used to measure stress, state/trait anxiety and anger, quality of life, and spiritual well-being in a convenience sample (N=42) of hospital workers completing a *mantra* intervention program.

  Result: Significant improvements were found in stress ($p < .001$), trait-anxiety ($p = .002$), trait-anger ($p = .02$), quality of life ($p = .001$), and spiritual well-being ($p = .003$). When examining the effects of *mantra* practice, anger, trait-anxiety, religious and spiritual well-being were significant ($p < .05$).

- A Spirituality based group intervention was conducted to assess the feasibility, effect sizes, and satisfaction of *mantra* repetition.

(Borman JE et al, Journal of Holistic Learning: Official Journal of the American Holistic Nurses Association, 2008, 26 (2):109-116)

The spiritual practice of repeating a sacred word/phrase throughout the day -- for managing symptoms of posttraumatic stress disorder (PTSD) in veterans.

Result: The study concluded that the spiritual program was feasible for veterans with PTSD who reported moderate to high satisfaction and symptom improvement.

THE POWER OF GAYATRI MANTRA

No other *mantra* of the Vedas is as glorious as the *Gayatri mantra.* All the Vedas, *yajnas*, charities, austerities etc. put together are a mere shadow of the all-powerful *Gayatri.* (*Rishi Vishwaamitra)*

Meditation, a 2500 year old practice in India, is a means to see things as they really are. It is not only India's one of the most ancient techniques, but also a universal remedy for curing universal ills.

Amongst the eight different kinds of meditation, namely- *Vipassana, Zazen, Kundalini,* Transcendental Meditation, Qi gong, Guided visualization, Trance-based practices and Heart Rhythm Meditation, *Gayatri* meditation is said to be the most effective as it is based upon the *Gayatri Mantra* - an ancient Vedic *mantra* mentioned in the Rig Veda.

> Meditation and reciting Mantras has immense influence on our Inner Self and its positive energy manifests itself both on our physical and our psychological well-being. Evolved more than 2500 years ago in India, it is a means to see things as they really are.

Considered to be the most powerful, the chanting of the 24 letters of the *Gayatri Mantra* activates energies in the subtle nerves of the tongue, throat, palate and the brain centre. Latent energies of the Chakras also get activated, which benefit the devotee both materially and spiritually.

Om Bhur Bhuvah Svah
Tat Savitur Varenyam
Bhargo Devasya Dheemahi
Dhiyo Yo Nah Prachodayat

Om *- Para Brahman;* ***Bhur*** *- Bhuloka (Physical Plane);* ***Bhuvah*** *- Antariksha;* ***Svah*** *- Svarga Loka;* ***Tat*** *- Paramatma;* ***Savitur*** *- Isvara (Surya);* ***Varenyam*** *- Fit to be worshipped;* ***Bhargo*** *- Remover of sins and ignorance;* ***Devasya*** *- Glory (Jnana Svaroopa);* ***Dheemahi*** *- We meditate;* ***Dhiyo*** *- Buddhi (Intellect);* ***Yo*** *- Which;* ***Nah*** *- Our;* ***Prachodayat*** *- Enlighten.*

BHAVA-ARTHA

"Let us meditate on *Isvara* and His Glory who has created the Universe, who is fit to be worshipped, who is the remover of all sins and ignorance. May he enlighten our intellect."

The aspirant prays to Mother Gayatri, "O Beloved Mother! At the present moment I have taken my body as the self-owing to *Avidya* or ignorance, through my impure intellect. Give me a pure intellect which will enable me to know my real nature. Give me light and knowledge."

This is the *Brahma-Gayatri Mantra. Gayatri* is the 'Blessed Mother' of Vedas. There is no milk superior to cow's milk. Even so, there is no *Mantra* superior to *Gayatri*. As *Omkara* or *Pranava* is for *Sannyasins*, so is *Gayatri* for *Brahmacharis* and householders.

> The aspirant prays to Mother Gayatri, "O Beloved Mother! At the present moment I have taken my body as the self-owing to *Avidya* or ignorance, through my impure intellect. Give me a pure intellect which will enable me to know my real nature. Give me light and knowledge."

The fruits that are attained by meditation on *Omkara* can be attained by meditation on *Gayatri*. The same goal that is reached by a *Paramahamsa Sannyasin* can be reached by a *Brahmachari* or a householder by meditating on *Gayatri*.

TECHNIQUE OF JAPA / MEDITATION

Get up at 4 a. m. in *Brahmamuhurta* and start *Japa* and meditation on *Gayatri* (*Panchmukhi* or five-faced *Devi* seated in lotus flower), sitting on *Padmasana, Siddhasana or Virasana,* facing North or East. Burn incense in the room. In summer you can take a bath. In winter you can simply wash your face, hands and feet and do *achamana* only. Continue the *Japa* for two hours or more. Have another sitting at night between 7 and 8 p. m. Constantly feel that you are receiving light, purity and wisdom from *Gayatri*. This is important. Keep the image of the *Gayatri* at the *Trikuti*, the space between the eye-brows by closing the eyes and concentrate there, or keep the image in the lotus of the heart and concentrate there. You will have *Darshan* of *Gayatri*.

Ideally it is better if you do *Japa* of *Gayatri* 3000 to 4000 times daily. Your heart will be purified rapidly. If you are not able to do this number, you can do 1008 times daily. If you find it difficult to do this number also, do at least 108 times daily, 36 times at sunrise, 36 times at noon, 36 times at sunset. There is special, mysterious spiritual force or wonderful magnetic power at *Sandhi* or junction of the time, sunrise and sunset. The mind will be elevated quickly. It will be filled with *Sattva*. Concentration will come by itself without any effort at this time. If you find it difficult to get up at *Brahmamuhurta*, get up before sunrise.

In the *Gayatri Mantra* there are 9 names, viz.,

1. *Om*,
2. *Bhur*,
3. *Bhuvah*,
4. *Svah*,
5. *Tat*,
6. *Savitur*,
7. *Varenyam*,
8. *Bhargo* and
9. *Devasya*.

Through these nine names the Lord is praised. *Dheemahi* is worship of the Lord. *Dhiyo Yo Nah Prachodayat* is prayer. Herein there are five halts or stops viz., '*Om*' is the first stop; '*Bhur Bhuvah Svah*' the second; '*Tat Savitur Varenyam*' the third; '*Bhargo Devasya Dheemahi*' the fourth; and '*Dhiyo Yo Nah Prachodayat*' the fifth. While chanting or doing *Japa* of the *Mantra*, we should stop a little at every stop or halt.

Savita is the presiding deity of the *Gayatri Mantra*, Fire (*Agni*) is the mouth, *Vishwamitra* is the *Rishi* and *Gayatri* is the metre. It is recited in the investiture of sacred thread, practice of *Pranayama* and *Japa*. *Gayatri* is the same as *Sandhya*, and *Sandhya* is the same as *Gayatri*. *Sandhya* and *Gayatri* are identical. He who meditates on *Gayatri*, meditates on Lord Vishnu.

A man can repeat *Gayatri* mentally in all states while lying, sitting, walking etc. There is no sin of commission and omission of any sort in its repetition. One should thus perform *Sandhya* three times with this *Gayatri Mantra* every day, in the morning, noon and evening. It is the *Gayatri Mantra* alone that can be commonly prescribed for all the Hindus. The Lord commands in the Vedas "Let one *Mantra* be common to all" "*Samano Mantrah.*" Hence the *Gayatri* should be the one *Mantra* for all the Hindus. "The secret lore of the Upanishads is the essence of four Vedas, while *Gayatri* with the three *Vyahritis* is the essence of the Upanishads." He is the real *Brahmin* who knows and understands thus, the *Gayatri.* Without its knowledge he is ignorant even though well versed in the four Vedas.

Repetition of *Gayatri Japa* brings the *Darshan* of *Gayatri* and eventually leads to the realisation of the *Advaitic Brahman* or unity of consciousness, or oneness (*Tanmayata, Talleenata, Tadrupata, Tadakarata*) and the aspirant who asked for light from *Gayatri,* in the beginning, sings now in exuberant joy, "I am the Light of lights, that gives light to *Buddhi.*"

May *Gayatri,* the Blessed Mother of Vedas, bestow on us right understanding, pure intellect, right conduct and right thinking! May She guide us in all our actions! May She deliver us from the *Samsaric* wheel of births and deaths! Glory! Glory unto *Gayatri,* the creatress, the generatrix of this Universe!

BUDDHISM ON ANGER

Chapter 3

Buddha is looked upon as a symbol of compassion, love, knowledge, same-sightedness, non-violence, equanimity, and peace. Also known as Siddhartha Gautama, Buddha, was a sage on whose teachings Buddhism was founded.

Born in the Shakya republic in the Himalayan foothills, he is believed to have lived and taught mostly in eastern India sometime between the sixth and fourth centuries BCE.

The word Buddha means "awakened one" or "the enlightened one". "Buddha" is also used as a title for the first awakened being in an era. In most Buddhist traditions, Siddhartha Gautama is regarded as the Supreme Buddha (Pali *sammasambuddha,* Sanskrit (*samyaksa buddha*) of our age.

Gautama taught the middle way between sensual indulgence and the severe asceticism found in the *Sramana* (renunciation) movement common in his region. He later taught throughout the regions of eastern India such as Magadha and Kosala.

In the face of anger, Buddha always manifested serene rationality, calmness of temper, generosity of heart, superb courtesy and gentle firmness. He was always healing people sick with exploding anger. He did not take it for granted that the angry person might not have a reason deserving respectful and searching consideration.

BUDDHA SUTTA

There are three main unwholesome (*akusala*) thoughts operating the human mind; *Lobha* (greed), *Dosa* (hatred) and *Moha* (delusion). These thoughts are put into action by the three-*kamma* doors (*dvara*); the mind, body and words. When thoughts come rushing in, these doors are activated. *Avega* is thoughts that come rushing in, and you lose control of these thoughts due to its speed. These unwholesome thoughts in man, with no internal control, lead to immoral action, words and thoughts.

Due to these *Lobha, Dosa, Moha* thoughts, some people demonstrate hatred without any fear. They get angry, fight in public, and do evil because they do not consider hatred as a shameful act. Some even try to justify this anger, while some openly talk and

> In the face of anger, Buddha always manifested serene rationality, calmness of temper, generosity of heart, superb courtesy and gentle firmness. He was always healing people sick with exploding anger.

laugh about what they did and said in anger. This shows that, either they are not ashamed of this action or do not realize that it is an inappropriate conduct.

Honestly, a person acting with hatred is a reason for you to be ashamed of. Human beings have the capability of controlling their thoughts and conducting themselves appropriately. Having this capability, immoral thoughts and conduct is unacceptable from any human being. Each time he is unable to control his unwholesome thoughts, he falls into the category of an animal. This is preventable. In order to overcome this situation, you need to control your anger and related unwholesome thoughts.

BUDDHA BHASHITA DISCOURSES

Buddha Bhashita discourse consists of *Aghata Pativinaya Sutta* and *Shravaka Bhashita*. The second discourse is preached by Arahant Sariputta which is the Second Aghata Pativinaya Sutta.

Aghata denotes rage, while *Pati* means completely and *Vinaya* means discipline.

Aghataya (Anger) is an emotion inculcated in the human mind. One may ask, "Why do we get angry? And what is the rationale behind this?" To this we can easily make an excuse saying so and so assaulted us or scolded us, but when we finally analyse these questions, the only logic that perfectly describes the situation is, anger arises only due to two reasons. The first is, not getting what you desire, while the other is, getting what you do not desire. These are the only two reasons why we get angry. Although we come up with various other explanations, everything finally boils down to the above-mentioned reasons.

NAWAGATA AND WAYS TO CONTROL ANGER

We get angry when we are unable to get what we want. This is human nature. But what if there is no one on whom we can vent out this anger? What do we do next? Start crying?

Crying is a *wanchaka* (fraudulent) *dhamma*. That means, expressing anger as an acceptable deception. It is not an admirable thing instead it is only a way of expressing anger. According to *dhamma*, there are nine ways of explaining anger, known as *Nawagata*. These include: a) Thinking about people and getting angry at those who have done injustice to you in past, present and future (3); b) Thinking same about people who may do the same to your near and dear ones in past, present and future (3); and c) Thinking about the same if they praise or help your enemies in past, present and future (3).

Anger builds up when things do not happen the way we anticipate. Therefore Lord Buddha has advised five ways of controlling this anger in the First Aghata Pativinaya Sutta .They are:

- **Develop *Metta* (loving-kindness):** Show loving-kindness to the person with whom you are angry. *Metta* means friendliness and friendship.
- ***Karuna* (Be compassionate):** What do you do if you get annoyed with a person? Show compassion, do not lose your temper or fight with him. What is compassion? It is a noble quality. When someone is crying and weeping in agony, helping to reduce his distress is compassion. Compassion is not getting together with that person and start crying.

- ***Upekka* (equanimity):** Equanimity is learning to think in a neutral way and remaining calm even during crisis. Most often, attachments make us sad. Stronger the attachment, the more miserable we become. Disagreements also cause unhappiness. Thus keeping a balanced mind at all times is advisable.
- **Stay without remembering or thinking:** Say, someone got angry due to a fault of another person. In such a situation, Lord Buddha's advice was to develop *"Asati Amanasikaraya"*. *Asati* means, stay without remembering and *amanasikaraya* is stay without thinking. If you get agitated because of a scolding or even thinking about it then disregard it and do not add any importance to it. Do not instil these thoughts into your mind. By keeping unwholesome thoughts in your mind and by adding value to it, you automatically become a slave to these thoughts.
- **Think of your own *kamma* (action):** Lord Buddha advices us to think of our own action, when we get annoyed or angry with a person. Depending on the wholesome or unwholesome deed (*kusal/akusal kamma*) a person does, he will face the consequences of it. Thereby, control your anger by thinking of your own *kamma*. The above five methods, advised by Lord Buddha, help a person in overcoming his anger.

LEADING BODHISATTVA'S WAY OF LIFE: SHANTIDEVA

Shantideva was born as a prince to King Kalyanavaram in India in 8th Century AE and later on became one of the greatest Buddhist monks. He is credited by his writings on patience and the concept of Bodhicaryavatara also referred to as the Way to Enlightenment.

Shantideva states in the very beginning of his chapter on patience that one moment of anger can wipe out a lifetime of merit. He says,

"Whatever wholesome deeds, such as venerating the Buddha's and generosity; that have been amassed over a thousand eons; will be washed away in one moment of anger."

When we get angry with someone we are often unaware of the effect it has on that person, let alone the ripple effect it causes. Nonetheless, it does indeed have a ripple effect: that person does not hang on to the anger but passes it on, perhaps repeatedly. The antidote to anger is patience.

A lack of understanding of patience, and its reflection in the overwhelming dominance of anger, has become endemic to our culture. Anger is one of the roots that cause so much unhappiness, suffering, discord, and violence in our world. It is expressed hundreds of times a day in the mass media, especially television. It is found in how we settle disputes in our highly litigious society; in how our leaders conduct themselves in the halls of Parliament /Congress; in the increase of domestic violence and child abuse; and in the sense of self-hating and self-loathing that pervades our culture. Politeness, kindness, patience, and compassion often seem a part of our mythical past.

THE CHALLENGE OF PATIENCE

How can someone maintain spontaneity and yet remain calm in his or her response during a situation which would ordinarily give rise to an outburst of anger? It is a challenge each one of us faces as we try to live our lives with a degree of human dignity and decency. At nearly every turn we are confronted with situations that test the limits of our patience and tolerance. Be it within our family, in the work environment, or simply when interacting with others, often our prejudices are revealed, our beliefs challenged, and our self-

> Most often, attachments make us sad. Stronger the attachment, the more miserable we become. Disagreements also cause unhappiness. Thus keeping a balanced mind at all times is advisable.

image threatened. It is in these moments that our inner resources are most called upon. All of this, Shantideva would say, tests our character, revealing how far we have developed our capacity for patience and tolerance.

Patience is something that cannot be cultivated in isolation from other people. In fact, it is a quality that can arise only within the context of our interaction with others, especially with fellow human beings. It is one thing to immerse oneself in warm thoughts of tolerance and compassion toward others in the unchallenged environment of solitude, but it is entirely a different matter to live these ideals in one's day-to-day interactions with real people. This is of course not to belittle the importance of silent meditation. Such solitary practices internalize insights, which otherwise would remain only at the level of intellectual knowledge. But the fact remains that the true test of patience comes only in the context of interaction with others.

By advocating the practice of patience, Shantideva is not suggesting that we should simply submit ourselves to abuse and exploitation from others. Nor is he recommending a policy of simple, unquestioned acceptance of suffering and pain. What he is advocating is a resolute stand against adversities. In his commentary, the Dalai Lama draws a distinction between meekness and tolerance. He suggests that genuine tolerance can only arise where one has consciously adopted a stance not to retaliate against an actual or perceived harm. The crucial point here is the "consciously adopted stand".

There is no evil like hatred and no fortitude like patience.
Thus one should strive in various ways, to meditate on patience.

"Patience", according to the Buddhist understanding of the principle, is "a resolute response against adversity stemming from a settled temperament unperturbed by either external or internal disturbance". Certainly, this cannot be described as a passive submission; rather it is an active approach toward adversity. Shantideva's discussion of patience takes place within the framework of what could be called the three characteristics of patience. They are: i) tolerance based on conscious acceptance of pain and hardships; ii) tolerance resulting from reflecting on the nature of reality; and iii) tolerance toward injuries from others.

He begins by observing that pain and suffering are natural facts of existence and that denying this truth can only cause additional misery. He then goes on to argue that if we could internalize this fundamental truth of our existence, we would derive enormous benefit in our day-to-day life. For one thing, we would see suffering as a catalyst for spiritual growth. To protect ourselves against tropical diseases we often submit willingly to the pain of inoculations. In arguing that it is possible to train ourselves to accept greater pain than we are capable of now, Shantideva writes the following memorable lines:

There is nothing whatsoever that is not made easier through acquaintance.
So through becoming acquainted with small harms, I should learn to patiently accept greater harms. (Guide, VI: 14)

Shantideva asserts that it is our experience of suffering that awakens us from our spiritual slumbers. It is also suffering that enables us to identify with others' pain, thus allowing us to generate

Anger arises only due to two reasons. The first is, not getting what you desire, while the other is, getting what you do not desire. These are the only two reasons why we get angry. Although we come up with various other explanations, everything finally boils down to the above-mentioned reasons.

genuine compassion for them. Furthermore, it is suffering that instils within us the fear of evil so crucial for the religious person. Finally, it is our insight into suffering that reinforces our longing for spiritual freedom.

The causes of happiness sometimes occur, but the causes for suffering are many.
Without suffering there is no renunciation, therefore mind, you should stand firm.

The second aspect of patience is tolerance based on understanding the nature of reality. The main focus of Shantideva's argument here is demonstrating how actions of people and events are determined by a network of many factors. This is to underline the critical fact that many of the conditions which cause others to act in ways that are harmful to us are in fact outside their control.

The principle underlying the second aspect of patience is nothing but the fundamental Buddhist principle of dependent origination. In this view, nothing arises in isolation, for everything comes into being due to the aggregation of multiple causes and conditions. The insights into reality which give rise to greater tolerance toward events and others' actions can also vary in their depth.

Shantideva poses the following rhetorical questions:

What is there to obtain or lose?
Who is there to praise or insult?
When does joy and pain arise?
What is there to be happy or sad about?

On the surface, it may seem that Shantideva is advocating a form of apathetic equanimity. Shantideva is drawing our attention to the intimate link between attachment and strong emotions like anger. The more we are attached to something, the more likely it is to make us angry when we perceive a threat to that object of attachment. We can see that the deeper our appreciation for the complexity of the circumstances giving rise to an event, the greater our ability to respond to that event with a degree of calmness and tolerance.

Hence everything is governed by other factors and in this way nothing governs itself.
Having understood this, I should not become angry, with phenomena that are like apparitions.

There is no denying that for most of us the main object of our anger or frustration is often a fellow human. And, until we learn to interact with others in a way that is not tainted by strong negative emotions such as anger, no genuine development of patience can take place.

Shantideva teaches us that it is more appropriate to have

For Dalai Lama, hatred can have no virtue. It only eats the person from within and poisons his or her interactions with fellow human beings. In his words, "Hatred is the true enemy; it is the inner enemy."

compassion rather than anger toward those who cause harm to us. He suggests that those who cause harm to others are in some sense possessed. In other words, their actions stem from a state of ignorance. In fact, Shantideva asks us to go further and regard those who harm us, our enemies, as precious, for they alone give us the rare opportunity to practise tolerance.

He further asserts that there is no evil like hatred and that there is no fortitude like patience. In Shantideva's view, anger acts as the principal obstacle to the development of patience. In medical analogy, hatred is the poison and patience is the medicine that removes the poisonous toxins from within the mind. Shantideva identifies the two key elements in our attempts to overcome anger. First and foremost, it is important for us to have a profound appreciation for the negativity of anger. Of particular relevance is to reflect upon the destructive effects of generating anger. Second, Shantideva identifies the need to develop a deep understanding of the causal mechanism, which underlines the arousal of anger.

Shantideva makes the crucial observation that the "fuel" of anger is what he calls "mental discomfort". It is best understood as a pervasive, underlying sense of dissatisfaction, which need not be felt at the conscious level. It is that nagging feeling that something is not quite right. Shantideva seems to be suggesting that it is this underlying sense of dissatisfaction that gives rise to frustration. Once this causal nexus between dissatisfaction, frustration, and anger is understood, we can then appreciate the virtue of Shantideva's approach in dealing with anger. We can see that much of his approach is aimed at rooting out this underlying sense of dissatisfaction rather than engaging in a head-to-head confrontation with actual full-blown anger. This is the reason for Shantideva's emphasis on reflections, which aim to create stability of mind.

So when seeing a human enemy or even a friend,
committing an improper action; by thinking that such things arise from conditions,
I shall remain in a happy frame of mind.

Shantideva does not appear to make any distinction between anger and hatred in his discussion. However, Dalai Lama's commentary explicitly underlines this critical distinction. He observes that, in principle, it may be possible to accept what could be called a "positive anger". Anger as an outrage toward injustice done to others can often be an important catalyst for powerful altruistic deeds. However, he rejects such possibility with regard to hatred.

For Dalai Lama, hatred can have no virtue. It only eats the person from within and poisons his or her interactions with fellow human beings. In his words, "Hatred is the true enemy; it is the inner enemy." Perhaps we can say that the feature which distinguishes anger and hatred is the absence or presence of ill-will. A person can be angry without bearing any ill-will towards his or her object of anger.

If I became angry at the wielder I am actually harmed by his stick.
Then since he too is secondary, being in turn incited by hatred, I should be angry with his hatred instead.

A key principle is a belief in what could be called the plasticity of the mind, that is, an assumption of the mind's limitless capacity for improvement. Generally speaking, in this view the mind is perceived in terms of a complex, dynamic system where both cognitive and affective dimensions of the psyche are seen as an integrated whole. Both Buddhist and modern psychology agree on the harmfulness of mere suppression. The Buddhist approach is

Once this causal nexus between dissatisfaction, frustration, and anger is understood, we can then appreciate the emphasis on reflections, which aim to create stability of mind.

to get at the root so that the very basis for anger is undercut. In other words, Shantideva and Dalai Lama are suggesting ways of reorienting our character so that we become less prone to strong reactive emotions such as anger.

The motto is simple:

> *Discipline your mind. Likewise, it is not possible for me to restrain the external course of things; but should I restrain this mind of mine, what would be the need to restrain all else? (Guide, V: 13-14)*

This of course is reminiscent of the memorable verse from the Dhammapada in which the Buddha says:

> *Intangible and subtle is the mind that flies after fancies as it likes; wise are those who discipline their minds; for a mind well-disciplined brings great joy. (Verse 35)*

Who can argue with the sheer practicality of the following lines which Dalai Lama is so fond of quoting:

> *Why be unhappy about something if it can be remedied?*
> *And what is the use of being unhappy about something, if it cannot be remedied? (Guide VI: 10)*

Generally speaking, all the major religions of the world emphasise upon the importance of practice of love, compassion, and tolerance. They all state that compassion and love are the foundation of all the spiritual paths.

In order to enhance one's development of compassion and cultivate the potential for compassion and love inherent within oneself, what is crucial is to counteract their opposing forces. It is in this context that the practice of patience or tolerance becomes very important, because only through patience is one able to overcome the obstacles to compassion.

QUOTES FROM THE DHAMMAPADA

- He who curbs his rising anger like a chariot gone astray, him I call a real Charioteer; other people are but holding the reins.
- Let a man overcome anger by gentleness, let him overcome evil by good; let him overcome miserliness by liberality; let him overcome lies by truth.
- Anger activates our body, tongue and mind. And we can then hurt others; more so ourselves, by these means. Therefore we have these teachings:
    - Beware of bodily anger, and control your body. Give up the sins of the body. Practise virtue with your body.
    - Beware of anger of your tongue, and control your tongue. Having abandoned the sins of speech, practise virtue with speech.
    - Beware of the anger of the mind and control your mind. Give up the sins of the mind and practise virtue with your mind.

The normal propensity of the angry man is to injure the victim of his anger with his body, tongue and mind; hence these specific warnings. But the fact remains that the mind is the central agency for setting anger in action through other limbs. Hence it is important to cultivate such a state of consciousness that anger is not allowed to rise in the mind.

TEACHINGS OF THE METTA SUTTA

Controlling or overcoming anger which has arisen is certainly good. But it is better to have a mind from which only love and bliss flow to all creatures in every direction. This teaching is known as the Metta-Sutta, which was reportedly taught to Bimbisara, the Magadha king. Buddha taught that all people seeking the well-being of themselves and others should cultivate this disposition of universal love:

'May all beings be happy and secure, may they be happy-minded. Whatever living beings there are, either feeble or strong, either long or great, middle-sized, short, small or large, either seen or unseen, which live far or near, either born or seeking birth, may all creatures be happy-minded. Let no one deceive another, let him not despise another, in any place; let him not out of anger or resentment wish harm to another. As a mother at the risk of her life watches over her own child, so also let everyone cultivate a boundless (friendly) mind towards all.

'And let him cultivate goodwill towards all in the world, a boundless (friendly) mind, above and below and across, unobstructed without hatred, without enmity.

'Standing, walking or sitting or lying down, as long as he is awake, let him devote himself to this mind, this way of living they say is the best in this world.'

SIKHISM ON ANGER

Chapter 4

According to Sikh Gurus there are Five Enemies, "*Kam* (lust), *Krodh* (anger), (*Lobh*) covertness or greed, *Moh* (attachment) and *Ahankar* (pride). These are like five rivers of fire. Falling into them, one is burned."

Guru Arjan Dev ji provides a telling description of each of these enemies, referring them to psychic entities or persons that lead the mind astray. On Anger, he says:

Anger (Krodh), the basis of all strife,
In whom there is no tenderness!
All creatures in your power,
Act like monkeys made to dance.
Your company makes man debased,
And subject to death's punishments,
O protector of the weak.
Nanak, from anger save us all!
(Guru Granth Sahib ji,1358)

Essentially these 'five enemies' are psychic propensities of the self that either attract the person towards something (maybe an object or an action), or repel the person away from what is wholesome. They are better understood not as biological or primitive instincts, but as learned dispositions or habitual frames of mind that can take on a life of their own. If left unchecked, these propensities keep the individual in a state of restlessness. The person whose being is motivated by these five enemies will continue to disregard *Hukam* and in doing so will inscribe ego into his or her being, thereby perpetuating the cycle of attachment to one's own ego. Such a person is called *manmukh* (lit, self-willed).

The Sikh scripture stresses upon the need for realization of the *Dasam Duar (Tenth Door),* following God's ordinance or *Hukam (Divine Order),* and the necessity of going beyond the realm of three-strand nature *(Triguna maya).* "The whole universe," says Guru Arjan Dev ji, Nanak V, "is bound by action, good or bad" *(Guru Granth Sahib ji, 51).* However Guru Nanak Dev ji declares that "all forms, beings, greatness and lowliness, pain and pleasure, bounties and wanderings are subject to the indescribable *hukam*sind, there

> Because human beings have been gifted with a superior brain, their actions in accordance with the proper understanding of *Hukam* can lead to progressive spiritual growth deserving His *Nadar*.

is nothing outside the realm of *Hukam,*" *(Guru Granth Sahib ji, l)* and then adds that "*karma* determines the kaprd, i.e. body or birth we receive and that it is through *Nadar* (God`s grace or Divine grace) that one secures *Moksha*" *(Guru Granth Sahib ji, 2).* Because human beings have been gifted with a superior brain, their actions in accordance with the proper understanding of *Hukam* can lead to progressive spiritual growth deserving His *Nadar*. Human birth, therefore, is a precious gift and a rare chance for the individual soul. Guru Nanak Dev ji says: "Listen, listen to my advice, O my mind! Only good deeds shall endure, and there may not be a second chance." Now, while the Sikh understanding of the process clearly acknowledges the traditional Indian articulation as a backdrop, there are some very important differences. Indeed the difference between the traditional Indic (or Brahmanic) concept of *Karma* and the Sikh articulation of it, encapsulated within the linked terms *karam/nadar/hukum*, boils down to very different concepts of time. Accordingly the interlinked notions of *Karma, Nadar* and *Hukam* often appear in the same hymn, underscoring the essentially paradoxical unity between them:

The deeds you do won't help you in the end,
For you reap whatever you've sown.
There is no other to protect you then,
Besides the saving grace shown by the Lord.
(Ramkalin M5, p. 898)

In the writings of the Sikh Gurus, the Vedic notion of *Karma* is replaced by the term *Hukam*, the imperative that is inherent within the nature of existence.

Instead of *Karma*, the Gurus speak of *karam*, deeds or actions that are aligned either with or against the working of *Hukam*.

It also says that the path of devotion is the easiest and superior most of all the paths. It is superior to the path of Action (*Karma*), the path of Knowledge (*Gyan*). In the path of Knowledge and Action, there is the danger of inflation of one's ego, for they involve an element of pride. In Devotion there are elements of meekness, humility and service. The paths of Action and Knowledge cannot invoke the mercy of the Lord. A seeker who is full of humility and meekness leaves everything to the will of the Lord and worships Him with devotion.

> *'...Joining with the humble Saints, I sing Gurbani. I have obtained the supreme status; meeting with the Saints, the self-elect, I am blessed and adorned. Anger and attachment have left my body and run away; I have eradicated hypocrisy and doubt. The pain of egotism is gone, and I have found peace; my body has become healthy and free of disease. By Guru's Grace, O Nanak, I have realized God, the ocean of virtue.' (Guru Granth Sahib ji,773)*

So which is that knowledge, which is that quality, which is that gem that we should seek? Which is the garb that we should put on to win the Lord's favour?

In answer to this, Guru Arjan Dev ji, the third Guru, in the Adi Granth says, "That knowledge is humility, that quality is simplicity and that precision gem is the sweet tongue. The disciple can win the favour of the Lord by putting on the garb of all these three qualities." Therefore to obtain the mercy and grace of the Lord, the seeker's heart should be dyed in humility and poverty. When at His door, we renounce our ego and bow our head in humility, then our soul becomes pure and is saved from the fire of passion.

Likewise, Guru Arjan Dev ji says: "The Guru is a true friend who never leaves you. He is the destroyer of ignorance. Guru is the beneficent one who blesses you with the Lord's Name. He is the embodiment of peace, truth and wisdom. He is the philosopher's stone whose touch turns all that is base into gold. He is the destroyer of our sins and purifier of the sinner. Guru is the pilgrimage, the pool of nectar wherein all sins are washed away. Guru exists from the beginning of time through ages after ages. Meditating on the Name that the Guru gives, which is the Name of the Lord, one attains Salvation."

Guru Gobind Singh said: "I say, truly, hearken ye all! Those alone realise the Lord who followed the path of Love."

"O Nanak! One is saved only by holding tight to good deeds." *(Guru Granth Sahib ji, 147).* So anger is compared in Gurbani to a "river of fire" and as we all know, fire is destructive; it burns whatever it touches and brings pain and suffering. Also, once spread, it is difficult to control. So the Guru tells us how anger can bring pain and suffering to the person just like fire and also how it is difficult to control anger once it has spread.

Elsewhere the Guru says, "*Kama* and *krodh* dissolve the body as borax melts gold." *(Guru Granth Sahib ji, 932).* The Guru gives a clear warning that *Kama* (excessive desire or lust) and *Krodh* (anger) "dissolve" the body just like gold is melted when placed in borax. So just like acid melts away metal anger can melt away the body. This is an internal process of eating away the healthy body tissues.

Guru Ram Das ji warns: "Do not meet with, or even approach those people, whose hearts are filled with horrible anger." *(Guru Granth Sahib ji, 40).* The Guru goes as far as asking us to keep away from *Sangat* (company of people) who cannot control their anger.

Gurbani tells us that: When "the Name of the Lord dwells within the mind; egotism and anger are wiped away." (Guru Granth Sahib ji, 33). The importance of *Simran* — the constant remembrance of the Lord, the Creator — will wipe away the state of anger and the feeling of ego from the mind and bring peace and tranquillity. "*Krodh* is to be vanquished and eradicated." This is done through "humility and firm faith" in the Divine.

Guru Arjan Dev ji's prescription: "Do not be angry with any one; search your own self and live in the world with humility. Thus, O Nanak, you may go across (the ocean of existence) under God's grace." *(Guru Granth Sahib ji, 259).*

Shaikh Farid, a thirteenth-century Muslim saint whose compositions are preserved in the Sikh Scripture, says in one of his couplets:

"O Farid, do good to him who hath done thee evil and do not nurse anger in thy heart; no disease will then afflict thy body and all felicities shall be thine." *(Guru Granth Sahib ji, 1381-82).*

Righteous indignation against evil, injustice and tyranny is, however, not to be equated with *krodh* as an undesirable passion. Several hymns in the Guru Granth Sahib ji, particularly those by Guru Nanak and Kabir, express in strong terms their disapproval of the corruption of their day.

Further, the Guru tells us that: "Lust and anger are brought under control, when the breath does not fly around, wandering

The Guru says, "*Kama* and *krodh* dissolve the body as borax melts gold." *(Guru Granth Sahib ji, 932).* The Guru gives a clear warning that *Kama* (excessive desire or lust) and *Krodh* (anger) "dissolve" the body just like gold is melted when placed in borax, like acid melts away metal, anger can melt away the body.

restlessly. By controlling our breath and the state of mind, these negative emotions could be subdued." *(Guru Granth Sahib ji, 1395).*

DANGERS OF BEING SELF-CENTRED (*HAUMAI*)

As mentioned before, the five vices or enemies make us self-centered, and build barriers against God in our lives.

However, Guru Nanak reminds us in the first stanzas of his *Japji*, the 'five enemies' cannot be controlled through ascetic practices, ritual cleansing or by philosophically reflecting about them. Rather they must be regulated by inculcating and actively practising virtues such as wisdom (*gyan*), truthfulness (*sach*), justice (*niaon*), temperance (*sanjam*), courage (*nidar*), humility (*garibi, nimarta*) and contentment (*santokh*). Those who actively appropriate such virtues are able to inscribe *Hukam* into their very being as ego-loss. They actively resist saying 'I am' and instead balance this egotistical propensity by being able to say 'I am not', and thereby elevate themselves beyond the self-willed rationalist morality of societal norms (*manmukh*). Thus a true Sikh should live according to what the Gurus stipulated. They disapproved of self-mortification and non-action and pronounced ritualism as useless. They recommended a householder's life of activity and responsibility lived with humility, devotion and service guided by proper knowledge of *Hukama'nd* - submission to God's will.

Guru Amar Das ji says, "Stop the mind from running out through the nine portals and open the Tenth Door, which will lead you to your home. There the Divine Melody will ring day and night, and it is through the grace of the Master that you can hear it." (Adi Granth).

The human body is endowed with Nine Apertures *(Navdvaras)* or opening. They are: two eyes, two ears, two nostrils, mouth, anus, and urethra. All these are vital organs of living organism called the human being. The Pali Suttanipata (verse 199. in Khuddak

Nikaya, Vol. 1, p. 297) is perhaps one of the very first Indian texts which mentions the idea of nine `holes' in the body. "Ever from its nine streams *(Navahi Sotehi)* the unclean flows." The *Dasam Dvar* however opens inside the body and renders a hyper-physical service by taking the seeker beyond the bondage of embodied existence. According to the Sikh view of D*asam Dvar,* the tenth door opens into the abode of God, the Creator *(Guru Granth Sahib ji, 974),* but only for those who keep the five sensory organs under their control.

The tenth door is the door of enlightenment and it opens only when the door consisting of *Haumai* or Self-Centeredness is broken. It is taken for granted in Sikhism that the tenth door is the supreme state of the mind. It is that state of purified consciousness in which God is visible and all contacts with physical existence are cut off. It is called a being's own house *(Nij-Ghar),* that is to say, a being's real nature which is like light *(Joti Sarup).* One hears day and night the *Anahad Sabda* there when one dwells in one's own house through the tenth door *(Guru Granth Sahib ji, 124).*

God himself has established nine houses in the city of this body; the Invisible and Infinite dwells at the tenth house or tenth door *(Guru Granth Sahib ji, 1036).* Thus the Tenth Door can only be opened by God's will or *Nadar*. Inside the front (i.e. the body) is the tenth door, the house in the cavity *(Gupha Ghar)*; in this fort nine doors have been fixed according to Divine ordinance; in the tenth door the Invisible, Unwritten, Unlimited Person shows Himself *(Guru Granth Sahib ji ,1033).*

A Sikh is called upon to seek, knowledge spiritual as well as secular, mundane and moral, practise *bhakti,* loving devotion, while leading a normal life of a *Gurmukh* or one whose face is turned towards the Guru. His actions should be guided by the ability to judge well which comes from the supreme knowledge along with dedication and complete self-surrender of a *bhakta.* Actions should be performed earnestly and honestly, doing full justice to his worldly duties. Yet he should not let himself be so much attached and entangled in the bonds of present life as to ignore the hereafter and to forget his ultimate goal which is reunion of his individual soul with its original source, the Supreme Spirit. Such actions help annihilate man's *Haumai* and, when blessed by God's *Nadar*, he can overcome the effect of past *Karma* and become *jivan Mukta*, i.e. one liberated while still living.

SIKH CONCEPT OF GOOD AND EVIL

The word good has relatively little meaning in Sikh ethics unless it is understood in relation to the problem of self-centeredness. Thus one might be deemed good in the sense that one diligently follows one's value or belief system which may or may not be associated with a particular set of life rules or code of conduct (*rahit*). And this may indeed involve respect or tolerance towards others. But according to *gurmat* (the Guru's philosophy) one might still be a *manmukh* (self-centered individual), whereas the aim in *Sikhi* is to achieve the state of consciousness known as *gurmukh*-one who has experienced self-realisation or Oneness by shattering his or her ego. This is therefore no essential goodness or badness. It is more accurate to speak of good and bad actions. For a *gurmukh* dualities such as 'good' and 'bad' have only relative meaning. To become a *gurmukh* one has to undergo self-transformation by overcoming the five psychic vices as mentioned above.

JAINISM ON ANGER

Chapter 5

Jainism, traditionally known as Jaina *dharma*, is an Indian religion that prescribes a path of *Ahimsa* or non-violence towards all living beings, and emphasizes spiritual independence and equality between all forms of life. Practitioners believe that non-violence and self-control are the means by which they can obtain liberation.

The word 'Jain' comes from the word 'Jina' which means a conqueror. 'Jina' comes from the root 'Ji'- to conquer passions. The passions are considered as enemies of the soul because they taint the natural qualities of the soul, obscure right belief, cause false knowledge and wrong conduct. Lust, anger, pride and greed are considered as the major passions.

In Jainism, *Kashaya* (Passion) is an aspect of a person that can be gained during his or her worldly life. According to the Jaina religion as long as a person has *Kashayas*, they will not escape the cycle of life and death. There are four different kinds of *Kashayas*, each being able to gain their own kinds of intensity.

These *Kashayas* are *Krodha* (Anger), *Mana* (Ego), *Maya* (Deceit), *Lobha* (Greed). These four can be grouped into two categories: 1) *Rag* (attachment) and 2) *Dwesh* (hatred). *Rag* is formed from *Maya* and *Lobha* and *Dwesh* is formed from *Krodha* and *Mana*.

KRODHA (ANGER)

When anger flares, we lose our sense of judgment. Virtues, love and forgiveness are destroyed. Anger arises if someone acts against our wish, if someone causes obstacles in the fulfilment of our desires, or if someone makes a breach of our trust. Everyone wants to stay away from those who become angry easily.

Due to anger, friends become foes. No one wants to help an angry person, nor does anyone love him. Anger nourishes revenge and instead of an angry nature we should have a forgiving and peaceful nature. Not only is anger harmful in this life, but it can bring bitter consequences in our next lives too.

Sometimes, virtuous people become angry, but they immediately calm down and ask for forgiveness from the people with whom they became angry. We should do the same. Thus, by following their example the sin caused by anger would be removed. We should cultivate virtues such as forgiveness, penance, and repentance.

These *Kashayas* are *Krodha* (Anger), *Mana* (Ego), *Maya* (Deceit), *Lobha* (Greed). These four can be grouped into two categories: 1) *Rag* (attachment) and 2) *Dwesh* (hatred). *Rag* is formed from *Maya* and *Lobha* and *Dwesh* is formed from *Krodha* and *Mana*.

LOBHA (GREED)

A greedy person is not satisfied with what he has. To get more, the person may use all kind of means without caring for others. We should not forget that our gain is a loss of others. Greed does not let us give anything away, even to the needy people.

We should be content with what we have and only accumulate to meet our needs. We should develop the habit of helping others by offering what we have. Greed destroys peace and happiness while caring brings them back.

MANA (EGO)

One who is full of ego loses his sense of judgement and politeness. A proud man invites his own destruction. We can obtain knowledge only if we are humble. Humility brings good thoughts where there is no room for pride or ego. Humility is at the root of religion and it is rather difficult to develop religious feelings as long as ego exists.

MAYA (DECEIT)

Deceit is responsible for a dishonest life. Due to deceit one loses friends. Honesty helps to realize the truth. A deceitful person has little understanding of religion.

There are nine *No-kashayash* (pseudo-passions) which trigger our passions. They are: 1) *Hashya* — laughing or joking; 2) *Rati* — pleasure for sensual activities; 3) *Arati* — displeasure for sensual activities; 4) *Shoka* — sorrow; 5) *Bhaya* — fear; 6) *Jugupsa* — disgust; 7) *Prurushved* — cause of sexual desires for women; 8) Strived — cause of sexual desires for men; and 9) *Napumsakaved* — cause of sexual desires for both men and women.

Control over them is paramount to maintaining mental and spiritual stability.

In Jainism, there are five gateways of knowledge. First is the sense of touch which is the lowest form of life. However, there are two, three, four and five senses in the higher forms of life. The second source is study, while third being *Avadhi* or the psychic faculty through which more subtle things are known. The fourth is mind, knowing by which the mental process are known. The fifth is Absolute Knowledge.

DOCTRINE OF KARMA

The doctrine of Karma occupies a very prominent place in the Jain philosophy. A student of Jain Karma philosophy can trace any effect to a particular Karma. Those who by right faith, right knowledge and right conduct destroy all Karmas, attain perfection. They become divine and are called Jinas. Those Jinas who, in every age, preach the law and establish the order, are called Tirthankaras.

The Jain doctrines are summed up in the maxim '*Ahimsa Paramo Dharmah*' (Non-Violence is the Supreme Duty). *Ahimsa* is the foundational tenet of Jainism. Jainism always tends to protect and advance the interests of all kinds of living beings. The universal principals of Jainism are *Ahimsa* (non-violence), *Satyam* (truth), *Asteya* (non-stealing), *Brahmacharya* (self-restraint of all senses), and *Aparigraha* (non-possessiveness).

Right faith, right knowledge, and right conduct constitute the triple path to *Nirvana*.

According to Jain philosophy, all evils are due to *Raga* and *Dvesha* (attachment and hatred). All the rules of conduct are based on *Daya* (mercy). *Daya* has four forms: 1) performing a kind act without expectation of a return; 2) rejoicing at the prosperity of others; 3) sympathy with distressed people and reliving their afflictions, and 4) pity for the criminal.

Jainism preaches universal brotherhood and equality of all beings. It enjoins on all its followers the practice of the greatest self-control. The individual by his own efforts liberates all his latent qualities which are obscured by foreign elements. The state of purity or perfection is attained only in the human life through the triple jewels, viz., right faith, right knowledge, and right conduct. The liberated soul goes to the abode *Siddhakshetra* which is at the top of this world.

ISLAM ON ANGER

Chapter 6

Islam is an Arabic word which means Peace. It also means submission to the will of God, while accepting the revelation and commands of God. In Islam, the personal name of God is Allah.

There are five cardinal tenets of Islam. These include: (1) Oneness of God and the revelation of God's will to man through prophets, the last of the series being Holy Prophet Muhammad (*Sallallahu alayhi wa salaam / saws* - may Allah's blessings and peace be with him) (2) Prayer (3) Fasting (4) Alms-giving or charity and (5) Haj (pilgrimage to Mecca).

HOLY QURAN AND HADITH ON ANGER

According to the Holy Quran and Hadith - a collection of teachings, deeds and sayings of the Holy Prophet Muhammad (*Sallallahu alayhi wa salaam / saws* - may Allah's blessings and peace be with him), anger is a destructive fire and devastating to human beings. Anger is one of the evil whispers of *Shaytan*, which leads to so many evils and tragedies, of which only Allah (*Subhanahu Wa Ta'ala /swt* or Glory to Him, the Exalted) knows their full extent.

Once the Prophet (saws) passed by some people who were wrestling. He asked, "What is this?" They said: "So-and-so is the strongest, he can beat anybody."

The Holy Prophet (saws) said, "Shall I not tell you who is even stronger than him? The man who is mistreated by another and is able to control his anger, has defeated his own *Shaytan* and the *Shaytan* of the one who made him angry." *(al-Bazzaar, and Ibn Hajr said in Isnaad is saheeh. Al-Fath, 10/519)*

The Holy Quran says ' Who spend [in the cause of Allah] during ease and hardship and who restrain anger and who pardon the people - and Allah loves the doers of good' *3:134*.

These are the ones whose good character and beautiful attributes and deeds Allaah (swt) has mentioned, and whom people admire and want to emulate. One of their characteristics is that "when they are angry, they forgive." *(al-Shooraa 42:47).*

> The Holy Prophet (saws) says, "Whoever curbs his anger, while being able to act, Allah (swt) will fill his heart with certainty of faith." Therefore, the consequence for whoever does not curb his anger is that he or she will sooner or later feel its evil consequences.

For this reason Islam has a great deal to say about anger and its teachings precisely describe the means to control it and limit its harmful effects.

One of the differences that Allah (swt) has made between humans and animals is their "ability to make choices". Controlling anger is one of the foremost characteristics of the pious. It is important to deal with anger in a rational way and forgive the offender.

Prophet Muhammad (saws) says, "Whoever curbs his anger, while being able to act, Allah (swt) will fill his heart with certainty of faith."

Therefore, the consequence for whoever does not curb his anger is that he or she will sooner or later feel its evil consequences.

Anger is a destructive emotion, as a fire which destroys our well-being, consumes our good actions, repels our friends and dear ones, frightens our children and forces the angels to report bad actions for the Heavenly Records. This is a dangerous rough road and no-one is devoid of it and it brings one close to the wrath of Allah (swt).

However, the good news is that when you are ready to confront the evil kind of anger within your soul, then you have already taken the first decisive step in fighting it. The evil kind of anger can be overcome by understanding the teachings of Islam because when we deal with people, our transactions are actually with Him and not His creation.

To understand this better let's look at a few proverbs from Quran that deal with anger. These include:

- "And when the foolish address them (with bad words) they reply back with 'Salamaa' (peaceful words of gentleness)." *(Qur'an, 25:63)*
- "The believer does not defame, abuse, disparage, nor vilify." *(al-Tirmidhi, sahih)*
- "And be moderate in your pace and lower your voice; indeed, the most disagreeable of sounds is the voice of donkeys... But of the people is he who disputes about Allah (swt) without knowledge or guidance or an enlightening Book." *(Qur'an, 31:19-20)*

FOLLOWING ARE A FEW VERSES FROM HADITH:

On one occasion, the Prophet (saws) mentioned, "Some are quick to get angry and quick to cool down, one character making up for the other; some get angry slowly and take as much time to cool down, one character making up for the other; but the best of you are those who are slow to get angry and quick to cool down, and the worst of you are those who are quick to get angry and slow to cool down."

Further the Prophet (saws) said, "Beware of anger, for it is a live coal on the heart of the descendant of Adam. Do you not notice the swelling of the veins of his neck and the redness of his eyes? So when anyone experiences anything of that nature he should lie down and cleave to the earth" *(Al-Tirmidhi Hadith 5145).*

On the restraint of anger the Prophet (saws) said: "No one has swallowed back anything more excellent in the sight of Allah (swt), who is Great and Glorious, than anger, seeking to please Allah (swt), the most high." *(Al-Tirmidhi Hadith 5116).*

Once a man came to the Prophet (saws) and said, "Messenger of Allah (swt), teach me some words which I can live by. Do not make them too much for me, lest I forget." The Prophet (saws) said, "Do not be angry." *(Al-Muwatta Hadith 47.11)*

"Do not become angry and Paradise will be yours" *(a saheeh*

Be moderate in your pace and lower your voice; indeed, the most disagreeable of sounds is the voice of donkeys... But of the people is he who disputes about Allah (swt) without knowledge or guidance or an enlightening Book." *(Qur'an, 31:19-20)*

hadeeth, Saheeh al-Jaam', 7374. Ibn Hajr attributed it to al-Tabaraanee, al-Fath 4/465): Remembering what Allah (swt) has promised to the righteous (*muttaqeen*) who keep away from the causes of anger and struggle within themselves to control it, is one of the most effective ways of extinguishing the flames of anger. One of the ahaadeeth that describe the great reward for doing this is: "Whoever controls his anger at the time when he has the means to act upon it, Allah (swt) will fill his heart with contentment on the Day of Resurrection." *(al-Tabaraanee, 12/453, also Sahih al-Jaami', 6518)*

TEACHINGS ON ANGER MANAGEMENT

There are different strategies for handling anger, depending on the person and situation. If a person gets angry, then he or she should exercise *muhasabah* (holding the self accountable) for the mistakes committed, what led to them, and how to overcome them in the future. Examining the self and holding ourselves accountable is important training and a source of discipline and self-improvement.

In various Hadiths, the Holy Prophet (saws) teaches us methods that are helpful in dealing with anger issues. They include among many:

- ***Seeking refuge in Allah (swt):*** The Holy Prophet (saws) said, "I know a word, the saying of which will cause him to relax, if he does say it. In this regard The Holy Prophet (saws) said: "If a man gets angry and says, 'I seek refuge with Allah (swt) from Satan,' his anger will go away." (Saheeh al-Jaami'al-Sagheer, no. 695) .That is a simple question to yourself will go a long way in controlling anger, ask yourself "Why should I be angry? What Allah (swt) has willed has happened." When we seek refuge in Allah (swt), we should say the words with understanding and reflection, not simply recite the words.

- ***Changing your posture:*** The Holy Prophet (saws) said: "Anger is a burning coal. Don't you see your eyebrows wide and eyes reddish? So when one of you feel angry, sit down if standing and lie down if sitting." *(Abu Dawud Book Hadith 4764).* In other words, make yourself calm like the soil if you are still angry. The cause of wrath is heat, and its opposite is to lie on the ground and make the body calm and cool. It has been commented, "One who is standing is in a position to strike and destroy, while the one who is sitting is less likely to do that, and the one who is lying down can do neither. It is possible that the Holy Prophet (saws) told the angry person to sit down or lie down so that he would not do something that he would later regret. And Allah (swt) knows best." *(Sunan Abee Daawood, with Ma'aalim al-Sunan, 5/141)*
- ***Keeping quiet:*** The Holy Prophet (saws) said, "If one of you becomes angry then he should stay silent." (Imam Ahmad, al-Musnad, 1/329). This is an important practice because when we are angry our actions and speech may be disproportionate and unjust. A disciple has reported, 'I heard the Holy Prophet (saws) saying, "A person utters a word thoughtlessly (i.e., without thinking about its being good or not) and, as a result of this, he will fall down into the fire of Hell deeper than the distance between the east and the west." *(Arabic/Hadith 1514)*
- ***Ablution:*** Wudu (Islamic procedure for washing parts of the body using water, typically in preparation for formal prayers) can also be a shield against anger. The Holy Prophet (saws) said,

"Anger comes from the devil, the devil was created from fire, and fire is extinguished only with water. So when one of you becomes angry, he should make wudu." or ghusl, for cold water extinguishes fire. *(Sunan Abi Dawud 4784)*

- ***Du'aa':*** Du'aa' is always the weapon of the believer, whereby he asks Allah (swt) to protect him from evil, trouble and bad behaviour and seeks refuge with Him from falling into the pit of kufr or wrongdoing because of anger. One of the things that can help save him is: being fair at times of contentment and of anger. *(Saheeh al-Jaami, 3039).*

One of the du'aa's of the Holy Prophet (saws) was: "O Allah (swt), I ask You to make me speak the truth in times of contentment and of anger. I ask You not to let me be extravagant in poverty or in prosperity. I ask You for continuous blessings, and for contentment that does not end. I ask You to let me accept Your decree, and for a good life after death. I ask You for the joy of seeing Your face and for the longing to meet You, without going through diseases and misguiding fitnah (trials). O Allah (swt), adorn us with the adornment of faith and make us among those who are guided. Praise be to Allah (swt), the Lord of the Worlds."

CHRISTIANITY ON ANGER

Chapter 7

Christianity is a radiant way of life. Jesus has taught that God is Spirit and Omnipresent. He is the Father of all, is transcendental and has infinite love for all His creatures. The theological doctrine is the belief in the Fatherhood of God and brotherhood of man.

For God there are three persons viz. Father, Son and the Holy Spirit. That is the Trinity of Christianity. All men are brothers because they all are members of the God's family. Inward purity, meekness, forgiveness, returning good for evil and faith in God are the central teachings of Christianity.

Jesus with his divine vision had found that every man or woman, rich or poor, saint or sinner was the embodiment of the same undying spirit. His teachings were thus to make everyone realize their own spiritual nature. According to Him we have to remove the dust and dirt that covers us so that our spirit shines through. "The Kingdom of Heaven is within you." *(Luke 17:21).* Another great lesson is renunciation. By that He means being selfless or utterly unselfish because once you are that , the man within you dies and God alone remains: "Blessed are the pure in heart, for they shall see God" *(Matthew 5:8).*

CAIN AND ABEL

Christians believe that the first man to discover the destructive power of anger was Cain. Cain and his brother, Abel, were the first two sons of Adam. When these sons grew up, Cain became a farmer and Abel became a shepherd. Cain and Abel had been taught the right way to worship God. They knew that God required an offering of innocent animals as a sacrifice for their sins. But, when they came to worship God, only one brother was obedient to God.

Abel brought a lamb as his offering, but Cain brought fruit from his crops as his offering.

God accepted Abel and his offering, but He rejected Cain and his offering. As a result of this, Cain became very angry. He was angry at God and jealous of his brother. God warned Cain of the consequences of his anger. God's message to Cain was this: "Look out! Your anger is like a lion lying in wait outside your door. You must master your anger or it will master you." But Cain did not respond to God's warning. His jealousy of Abel turned into

> "Do not hasten in your spirit to be angry, for anger rests in the bosom of fools." *(Ecclesiastes 7:9).*

hatred. One day, as Cain and Abel were in the field together, Cain rose up against his brother and murdered him. Thus the first man born into this world became a murderer because he did not control his anger.

WHY THE ANGER?

Anger is within us but we must master it or it will master us. God has warned us of the dangers of uncontrolled anger. The Bible says, "Be angry, and do not sin; do not let the sun go down on your wrath." *(Ephesians 4:26).*

Anger is the most violent of human emotions. Because it involves such strong feelings, anger borders closely on sin. When anger is out of control, it does great damage. When we become angry, we want to lash out at someone and hurt them, we are sinning deeply. Losing our temper is a sign of weakness, not strength. The Bible says, "Do not hasten in your spirit to be angry, for anger rests in the bosom of fools." *(Ecclesiastes 7:9).*

DEALING WITH UNCONTROLLED TEMPER

Temper is uncontrolled anger. When we lose our temper, there is but one thing to do: Confess it to God as a sin. If we have offended or hurt others, we must apologize to them. In *Matthews 23 – 26,* Lord Jesus says that if you are offering a gift at the altar, and your brother has something against you, leave your gift there and go. Thereafter, reconcile with your brother, and then come and offer your gift. Make friends quickly with your accuser, while you are going with him to court, lest your accuser hands you over to the judge, and the judge to the guard, and you are put in prison; truly, I say to you, you will never get out till you have paid the last penny.

Regardless of how many times you lose your temper, you must make things right with others. This will humble you and help you see the damage done by your temper. At the same time, you must also deal with the cause of anger because until we do that we will keep doing the same thing over and over again.

So how do we do that? What are the causes of anger?

We may try hard to control our anger, but unless our senses are dealt with, we will continue to get angry.

So called common situations which hurt us and give rise to anger are like feelings of being 'belittled'. This happens when someone says something unkind or hurtful about us, or when we become angry on the inside. We also tend to feel belittled when we cannot have our own way, or when someone is honoured above us. Situations like these often result into jealousy, which soon turns into anger.

We may not realize it, but the main reason for all our discontent is that we love ourselves and want to please ourselves. So long as we make ourselves the centre of everything, we will react with anger and lash out at anyone who crosses us.

Because selfishness and ego is so hateful to God and so destructive to us, God did something about it. God dealt with it by putting Christ on the cross. When Christ was crucified, we were crucified with Him. He crucified us with Christ so that we might no longer be ruled by this sense of false self-pride or ego. The Bible says, "Knowing this, that our old man (our former self) was crucified with Him that the body of sin might be done away with that we should no longer serve sin." *(Romans 6:6 NKJB)*

Two great facts which are true of every Christian: (1) Christ died for us, (2) We died with Christ.

> "Let all bitterness, wrath, anger, clamour (loud quarrelling), and evil speaking be put away from you, with all malice." *(Ephesians 4:31)*

NEW TESTAMENT ON ANGER

In *Matthew 5:21-22,* Lord Jesus uttered the following words: "You have heard that it was said to the men of old, 'You shall not kill; and whoever kills shall be liable to judgment.' (21) But I say to you that everyone who is angry with his brother shall be liable to judgment; whoever insults his brother shall be liable to the council, and whoever says, 'You fool!' shall be liable to the hell of fire." (22)

While St James *(James 1:20)* says, "Anger can become sinful when it is motivated by pride, when it is unproductive and thus distorts God's purposes", Paul the Apostle in Ephesians believes that one should speak the truth in love and use words to build others up, not allow rotten or destructive words to pour from their lips.

St. Augustine believes that it is better to deny entrance to just and reasonable anger, than to admit to it, be it ever so little. "Once admitted, it is with difficulty driven out again. It enters as a little twig and in less than no time, it grows big and becomes a beam," says St. Augustine.

He adds, "The purport of this precept is that if the mind nurtures anger, it will manufacture out of it, hatred, which will be extremely difficult to get rid of. Anger is always well supplied with thousand false pretexts for nourishing it. There was never an angry man who thought that his anger was unjust."

St. Francis De Sales writes: "It is better to attempt to find the way to live without anger, than to pretend to make moderate and discreet use of it. When we find ourselves surprised into anger through our imperfections and frailty, it is better to drive it away speedily than to enter into a discussion with it. If you give it ever so little time, it will become the mistress of the place, like the serpent who easily draws in the whole body where he can once get in his hood."

MEEKNESS

Meekness, or forgiveness, is associated with the beatitude, "Blessed are the meek, for they shall inherit the earth" *(Matthew 5:5)*. Meekness is not weakness, but submission to God, motivated by love. Meekness combats the sin of anger in our lives. We know that Jesus was totally submissive to the will of the Father, and never gave in to sinful anger, as we see in the Scriptures. This is the kind of meekness that we need to aspire to.

WHAT IS MEEKNESS?

Meekness is a virtue that moderates anger and controls resentment toward others. It is finding strength through submission to God. Meekness helps us to keep our cool and remain ourselves in the midst of adversity.

According to De Sales, just like a farmer who fills his granary at the time of harvest, we too should build up a stock of sweetness and calmness deep down within our character when circumstances are propitious so that these become our involuntary habit pattern.

Most of us can behave in a correct manner when we are aware that we are being observed. But the true test of our character is noted when we are unaware that we are being observed. Unless we build up good habit patterns through conscious self-discipline, our inner weaknesses will show up embarrassingly, when we are off guard.

Though our spiritual failures can cause us some remorse, we are often warned to refrain from bitter, gloomy and cynical self-criticism. Because those who are overly angry with themselves,

> "Blessed are the meek, for they shall inherit the earth" *(Matthew 5:5)*. Meekness is not weakness, but submission to God, motivated by love.

only succeed in keeping their hearts soaked and steeped in passion, which makes the task of overcoming anger even more difficult. Therefore we should by all means rise up again after every fall, with a new resolve, meekly, humbling ourselves before God, through the knowledge of our own frailty.

St. Abba Dorotheus, one of the Desert Fathers, who lived between the 6th and 7th centuries, wrote in the 'Directions on Spiritual Training,' about the great efficacy of humility in overcoming anger.

He says, "Humility is neither angered, nor angers any one. Humility attracts God's grace to the soul; and God's grace, when it comes delivers the soul from these two grievous passions."

He questions, "For what can be more grievous than to be angry with one's neighbour or to anger him? Does humility deliver one from only two passions? It delivers the soul from every passion and every temptation and is of such great value in overcoming anger."

PRACTICAL STEPS TO CONQUER ANGER

WE MUST SEE IT AS OUR WEAKNESS

Many people when angry are in denial. Others admit that they have a temper, but do not see it as a serious sin. Actually, temper is one of the worst sins. The Bible lists uncontrolled anger along with such sins as drunkenness, witchcraft, adultery, and murder. *(See Galatians 5:19-21.)* Temper is simply not acceptable in the life of a

Christian. The Bible says, "Let all bitterness, wrath, anger, clamour (loud quarrelling), and evil speaking be put away from you, with all malice." *(Ephesians 4:31).* Unless we see the seriousness of our temper and determine to be delivered from it, we will not overcome it. If we are satisfied to go on as we have been going, we will know nothing of God's victory over the sin of temper.

WE MUST ACCEPT RESPONSIBILITY FOR OUR TEMPER

Blaming someone else for our temper is very easy. Many a times, we think that our temper is an external problem—that it is caused by something from without. The fact is that temper is an internal problem. Temper comes from within us, not from without. Others may say or do things that irritate us, but no one can make us lose our temper except us.

WE MUST COUNT ON THE SACRIFICE OF LORD CHRIST

God has told us plainly that He has delivered us from the power of sin by the death of Christ, that is, the Lord gave up his life for saving us. The Bible says, "Reckon yourselves to be dead indeed to sin (including the sin of temper), but alive to God in Christ Jesus our Lord." *(Romans 6:11).* We must put God's truth into practice. When we find ourselves getting angry or acting aggressively, we must try to convince ourselves that this is not the real me and my old angry self was crucified along with Christ. Thinking that Christ lives in you and that He is your life will calm the agitated mind and quell the feeling of anger.

WE MUST CONTROL OUR SENSES

Whether or not we lose our temper is not determined by what happens on the outside. It is determined by the one in control on the inside. Christ alone has the right to rule in our life, but our senses will still try to rule. Every Christian must choose whether he will be ruled by Christ or by their senses. It is God's purpose that Christ reign on the throne of our heart. In order for Him to reign, all senses must be kept in the place of death on the cross. It is one thing to understand the teaching that we were crucified with Christ. It is another to put it into practice and actually deny them. But this is what we must do. Jesus said, "If any man will come after Me, let him deny himself (deny Self), and take up his cross daily, and follow Me." *(Luke 9:23)*

CONFESSION

"If we confess to our sins, He is faithful and just and will forgive us and our sins and purify us from all unrighteousness." *(John 1:9)*

Confession is one of the best ways to handle anger. God knows us better than we know ourselves, and we will always find Him to be understanding. Being alone in God's presence can calm us down. It also helps us to see things in their proper perspective. Many times we discover that the things we were disturbed about were not really so important after all. Along with this comes atonement. If we have offended or hurt others, we must apologize to them. Regardless of how many times you lose your temper, one must make sincere effort to set things right with others each time. This will humble you and help you to see the damage done by your temper.

FOOD AND YOGA *ASANAS*

Chapter 8

According to Sri Shankaracharya the word 'food' means anything that is taken in by the senses, viz. sound, sight, smell, etc. Improper sensory inputs create attachment, aversion, and delusion, which disturb the mind, making it difficult to control. Freed from these, the mind becomes pure. In order to consciously bring about preponderance of *Saatva* in our nature, we need to allow only *Saatvic* inputs and avoid those that are *Rajasic* or *Tamasic*.

The Shankaracharya also believes that one half of the stomach should be filled with food including curries; the third quarter should be filled with water; but the fourth quarter should be left for the movement of air, etc.

Food is largely a matter of temperament. The Upanishad teaches: 'When the food is pure, mind becomes pure. When the mind becomes pure, memory becomes firm. And when a man is in possession of a firm memory, all the bonds which tie him down to the world are loosened.'

According to the Bhagavad Gita: 'Food also, which is agreeable to different men according to their innate disposition, is of three kinds. And likewise sacrifice, penance and charity too are of three kinds each; hear their distinction from Me.' *(Gita: 17.7)*

In the above verse the Lord invites Arjuna to hear the classification of food, sacrifice, penance and charity. Accordingly, He proceeds to describe in the following verse the *Saatvika* types of food, which are worth taking.

Foods, which promote longevity, intelligence, vigour, health, happiness and cheerfulness, and which are sweet, bland, substantial and naturally agreeable are dear to the *Saatvika* types of men. *(Gita: 17.8)*

Having mentioned the diet of *Saatvika* men, which deserves to be adopted by all, the Lord now describes in the following two verses the diet of *Rajasic* and *Tamasic* men, which should be shunned by all.

Food, which are bitter, acidic, salty, over hot, pungent, dry and burning, and which cause suffering, grief and sickness, are dear to the *Rajasic* type of men. *(Gita: 17.9)*

Food, which is half cooked or half ripe, insipid, stale and polluted, and which is impure too, is dear to men of *Tamasic* disposition. *(Gita: 17.10)*

> 'When the food is pure, mind becomes pure. When the mind becomes pure, memory becomes firm. And when a man is in possession of a firm memory, all the bonds which tie him down to the world are loosened.'
>
> – *Upanishad*

YOGA ASANAS

Yoga is a mind and body practice with historical origins in ancient Indian philosophy. Like other meditative movement practices used for health purposes, various styles of yoga typically combine physical postures, breathing techniques, and meditation or relaxation.

Yoga can help you relax and de-stress the body when anger flares up. It is important to understand that anger should not be repressed; instead one should allow oneself to experience the emotion. However, instead of reacting in destructive ways, it is important that a person channelises his energy into yoga poses.

However, always, check with your doctor if you are pregnant or have other concerns.The following *Asanas* are particularly helpful in calming the mind and stabalising it.

SHEETALI PRANAYAMA

Pranayama is controlling the *Prana* or breath. In *Raja* Yoga, breathing enters the psychic plane and brings us to the spiritual. It is the fly-wheel of the whole bodily system.

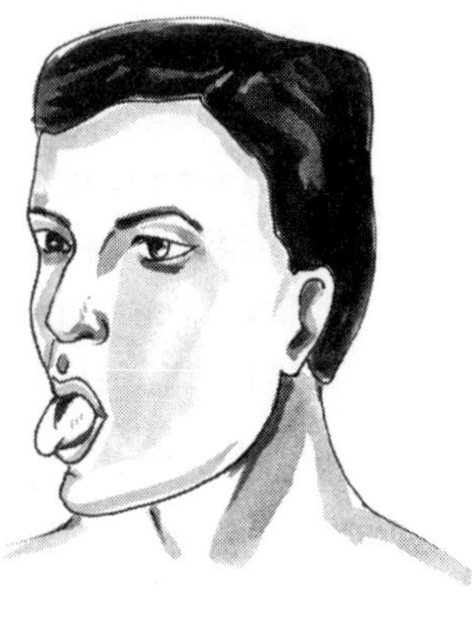

Pranayama has three parts:

1) *Puraka*: inhaling
2) *Kumbhaka*: restraining
3) *Rechaka*: exhaling

Sheetali Pranayama is Yoga's answer to heat, stress, anger and irritation. *Sheetal* means calmness and peacefulness and those are the results of practicing this cooling breath. It is usually done after practising other *asanas* and *pranayamas*. *Sheetali pranayama* is mentioned in the yoga texts *Hatha Yoga Pradeepika* and *Gheranda Samhita*.

Sheetali involves folding of the tongue to form a tube like shape. Some people may find it difficult to fold their tongue. They can do an alternate practice call *Sheetkari Pranayama*, which gives similar benefits.

Avoid doing *Sheetali pranayama* if you are suffering from a cold as it is counterproductive. But if you are in a hot environment, it is ideal for cooling the body.

BENEFITS OF *SHEETALI PRANAYAMA*

- The action of pulling the air through the tongue creates a cooling effect on the body.
- *Sheetali* relaxes the body and the mind.
- According to *Hatha* Yoga *Pradeepika, Sheetali* can cure colic, enlarged speen, fever and disorders of the bile.
- *Sheetali* can also remove hunger and thirst.

DESCRIPTION OF THE *ASANA*

- Sit in a comfortable *asana* with palms on the knees.
- Roll the tongue from the sides so that it forms a narrow tube. The tongue is folded from both the sides and the edges almost meet at the center on the top.
- Breathe in slowly. First fill the abdomen, then the chest and finally the neck region. This is the complete *yogic* breath.
- Pull the tongue inside the mouth and close the mouth.
- Bend the neck forward to do the chin lock, also called the *Jalandhara Bandha*.

Yoga can help you relax and de-stress the body when anger flares up. It is important to understand that anger should not be repressed; instead one should allow oneself to experience the emotion.

- Hold the breath for some time, as long as you are comfortable
- Release *Jalandhara Bandha* and exhale slowly through the nose.

This is one round of *Sheetali Pranayama*. One can do as many rounds as one may feel comfortable with.

SARVANG ASANA (THE SHOULDER STAND)

BENEFITS OF *SARVANG ASANA*

- Effective for excessive anger or hate, migraine headache, liver disorder, haemorrhoids, anaemia, hypertension, indigestion.
- The shoulder stand invigorates and rejuvenates your whole body.

DESCRIPTION OF THE *ASANA*

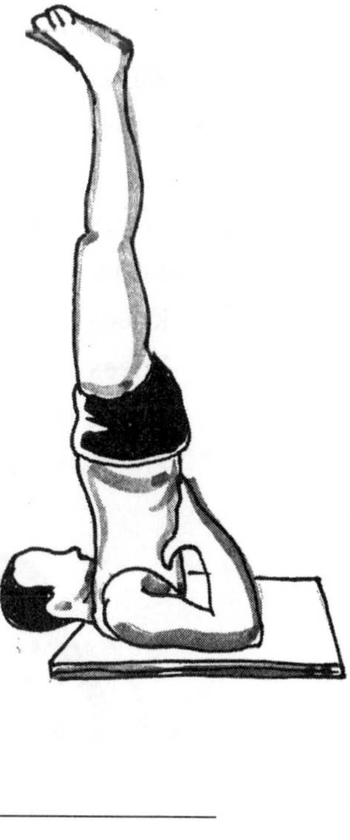

- Lie down on the floor with your legs together a your hands, push down, by your sides. Inhalii push down on your hands and raise your le straight up above you.
- Lift your hips off the floor and bring your legs over and beyond your head, at an angle of about 45°.
- Exhaling, bend your arms and support your body, holding as near the shoulders as possible,

thumbs around the front of the body, fingers around the back. Push your back up, lift your legs.

- Now straighten your spine and bring the legs up to a vertical position. Press your chin firmly into the base of your throat. Breathe slowly and deeply in the pose, gradually trying to work your elbows closer together and your hands further down your back toward the shoulders, so as to straighten your torso. Keep your feet relaxed.

CAUTION

- Shoulder stands should not be attempted without a qualified teacher.
- Any one suffering from breathing difficulties or pain in the upper spine should not attempt these postures.

GUPTA PADMASANA (HIDDEN LOTUS POSE)

BENEFITS OF *GUPTA PADMASANA*

This asana corrects postural defects of the spine. It may be used as a relaxation or even a meditation pose as it induces peace, stability and emotional balance.

DESCRIPTION OF THE *ASANA*

- Sit in *Padmasana*. Place the hands on the floor in front of the knees. Leaning on the arms, raise the buttocks and stand on the knees. Slowly lower the front side of the body to the floor in the prone position. Rest either the chin or one cheek on the floor.
- Place the palms together behind the back. The fingers may point

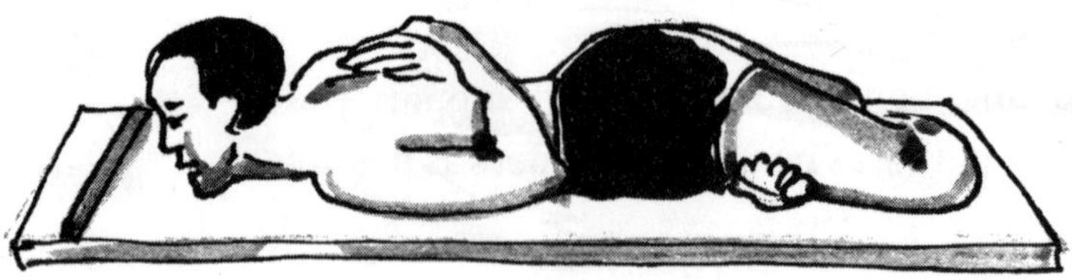

downward, or upward in Universal Spirit. If possible, touch the back of the head with the middle fingers. Close the eyes and relax the whole body.

- Return to the starting position, cross the legs the other way and repeat the *asana*.
- Hold the position for as long as is comfortable. For complete relaxation, the hands may rest on the floor beside the body with the palms upward.

SHAVASANA (THE CORPSE POSE)

BENEFITS OF *SHAVASANA*

The goal of the *Shava-asana* is to keep the body and mind perfectly still and relaxed. Not only should the body be motionless and at ease, but the mind as well should be quiet, like the surface of a still lake. The result will be a deep and stable relaxation that will extend into your meditation or be felt through the activities of your daily circumstances. If you find yourself getting drowsy while in the Shava-asana increase the rate and depth of your breathing.

DESCRIPTION OF THE *ASANA*

- Lie flat on your back with your legs together but not touching, and your arms close to the body with the palms facing up.
- Keep your eyes gently closed with the facial muscles relaxed and breathe deeply and slowly through the nostrils.
- Starting at the top of the head and working your way down to the

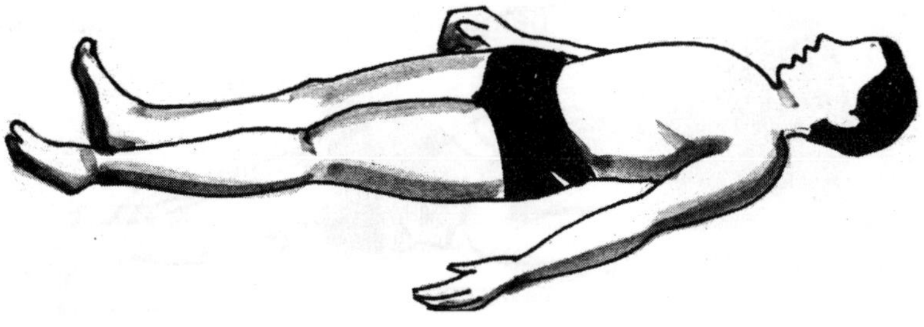

feet, bring your attention to each part of your body, consciously relaxing it before proceeding on to the next.

- Remain in the *Shava-asana* for between 3 and 5 minutes or longer. If you become sleepy, while in the *Shava-asana* begin to breathe a bit faster and deeper.

SHASHANKASANA (RABBIT POSE)

BENEFITS OF THE ASANA

It's *asana* helps control anger and when you get used to doing this *Asana*, anger will remain under control in future. Peace of mind will be achieved and it will help in concentrating on work or studies and it's good for sound sleep. This pose also helps remove gas from the abdomen, while pain in waist, lower back and neck will be reduced.

DESCRIPTION OF THE ASANA

- Sit in *Vajrasana* with both hands folded behind your waist.
- Now catch hold of one wrist with other palm.
- Start exhaling air and slowly bend forward and try to touch forehead to ground.
- Do not lift your buttocks off your ankles while doing this.
- Stay for 20 breath counts (at least 10 in beginning stages) and then slowly inhale and come back to original position of *Vajrasana*.
- You may not bend completely in first attempt, so try to bend as much as possible and practise it a few times every day till you

can bend completely. While bending, concentrate on your head going down.

- Next, stretch both your arms above your head and continue with bending down.
- After repeating this for 10 times stretch both arms towards sideways and bend down.
- While bending, concentrate on your chest.
- In next step, interlock both hands behind your neck and start bending and touch the ground with your forehead.
- Concentrate on your neck, while bending.
- After repeating this 5-10 times, now interlock both your palms at your back and bend your head forward as in the picture above.
- When head touches ground, try to lift your waist and try to touch your feet with your palms.

THE POWER OF MUSIC

Chapter 9

Philosophers and sages throughout the ages have asserted the decisive influence music can have on the character and moral formation of the young and on the formation of a civilization.

Music according to Hindu scriptures is *Gandharva Vidya* and the most ancient of arts. *OM* is *Nada Brahman*. *Nada* is sound. Sound is vibration and *OM* is the first vibration of sound thus it is the first manifestation of the absolute. It is the comprehensible basis for all creation. As *Brahman* is incomprehensible in Its transcendental aspect, the nearest approach to It is sound, so it is also called *Apara Brahman*. Ravana, it is said, propitiated Lord Shiva through music.

In the 6th Century, the Christian philosopher Anicius Boethius wrote: "Music can both establish and destroy morality. For no path is more open to the soul for the formation thereof than through the ears. Therefore, when the rhythms and modes have penetrated even to the soul through these organs, it cannot be doubted that they affect the soul with their own character and conform it to themselves."

Boethius attested to the awareness that ancient peoples had about the influence of music. So great was the regard for music among them, that they looked on it as having a definite power over the soul.

Music, as it brings us and unites with God is thus and is called *Nada* , an ancient Indian metaphysical system. Music, thus, should not be regarded as an instrument for titillation of the nerves or satisfaction of the senses only; it is a *Sadhana,* which enables you to attain *Atma-sakshatkara*. It is the foremost duty of all musicians, and institutions interested in the promotion of music, to preserve this grand ideal and this pristine purity that belongs to music.

It is both a philosophical system, a medicine, and — as the name suggests — a form of yoga. The system's theoretical and practical aspects are based on the premise that the entire cosmos and all that exists in the cosmos, including human beings, consists of sound vibrations, called *Nada*. This concept holds that it is the sound energy in motion rather than of matter and particles which form the building blocks of the cosmos.

OM is *Nada Brahman*. *Nada* is sound. Sound is vibration and *OM* is the first vibration of sound; thus it is the first manifestation of the absolute. It is the comprehensible basis for all creation.

Nada yoga is also a way to approach with reverence and respond to sound. Sound and music is in this context, something more than just the sensory properties and sources of sensuous pleasure. Sound and music is considered also to play the role as a potential medium to achieve a deeper unity with both the outer and the inner cosmos.

Nada yoga's use of sound vibrations and resonances are also used to pursue palliative effects on various problematic psychological and spiritual conditions. It is also employed to raise the level of awareness of the postulated energy centres called *Chakras*.

FROM WHERE HAS MUSIC DERIVED THIS MIGHTY POWER?

Music is derived from the supreme music of *Brahman*, the sacred *Pranava*. Music is intended to reverberate this *Pranava-Nada* in your heart. Therefore you love to hear music, which is but the most melodious intonation of your own essential name. When the mind thus gets attracted and gets unified with one's essential nature the great power of God stored up there wells up within and heals body and mind. That's why all of us love music. Though it may originate from different cultures or maybe we don't even understand the words; because the basic foundation of sound is the same, it touches the heart.

STAGES OF SOUND

The Vedas form the sound-manifestation of *Ishwara*, the non-decaying reality. This sound has four divisions: 1) *Para* which finds manifestation only in *prana*, 2) *Pashyanti*, which finds manifestation in the mind, 3) *Madhyama*, which finds manifestation in the senses, and 4) *Vaikhari*, which finds manifestation in articulate expression. These four are the various gradations of sound. They are the gradual and materialized expressions of the transcendental voice. The Lord manifests Himself through His power of *maya* first as *para vani* in the *mooladhara chakra* at the perineum, then as *pashyanti* in the *manipura chakra* at the navel, next as *madhyama* in the heart and then eventually as *vaikhari* in the throat and mouth. This is the divine ascent of voice.

PARA VANI

The highest manifestation of sound energy, the primal voice, the divine voice is *para*. The *para* voice gives birth to root ideas or germ thoughts. It is the first manifestation of voice. In the *para* state the sound remains in an undifferentiated form.

PASHYANTI VANI

Yogis who have subtle inner vision experience the *pashyanti* state of sound. Sound is associated with colour, form and accordingly the *pashyanti* state of sound is an object of internal vision. Thats the reason it is called *pashyanti* (from the root *pashyat*, one who sees).

Music, thus, should not be regarded as an instrument for titillation of the nerves or satisfaction of the senses only; it is a *Sadhana,* which enables you to attain *Atma-sakshatkara.*

The more we trace the inner origin of different languages, the more we are approaching the vibrating homogeneity of sound behind them. Birds, beasts, Indians, Africans, Americans — all experience the same feeling of a thing in the *pashyanti* state of sound. As one and the same *shakti* working through ears becomes hearing, through the eyes becomes seeing, and so forth, so also the same *pashyanti* experience assumes different forms of sound when materialized.

MADHYAMA VANI

Madhyama is the intermediate unexpressed state of sound experienced in the heart.

VAIKHARI VANI

Vaikhari is well known to us. It is the articulated sound, the last and grossest expression of divine sound energy. However, all *vaikhari* sounds are His voice only. It is the voice of the *Virat Purusha*. He as *paratpara*, the transcendental, stands beyond and above all states of consciousness and sound, and with mere will sets the vibrations of sound in motion to extend them on to the grosser planes. To us on the physical plane, this divine voice of His is known as *vaikhari* or the physical speech.

MUSIC OF THE SPHERES

The divine voice is expressed in the lower planes in the above four ways. But there is another expression of His voice: the music of the spheres. This is created by the rotation of the whole universe, the earth, moon, sun, stars, satellites, etc. Like the sweet humming sound of a top set in brisk motion, all these bodies similarly rotate on their own axis, and thereby the music of the spheres is created. This, too, is His voice.

Though inaudible to human ears, it exists at all times and everywhere. Sages and yogis can hear it. If the heart is simple and receptive, you too can catch the subtle vibrations of that universal sound.

INFLUENCE OF MUSIC OVER MIND AND BODY

Sweet melody exercises a powerful influence on the mind and physical nature of every living being. Trapped in music, the mysterious mind with its thousand hoods of *Vasanas* and *Vrittis*, lies quintescently on the lap of the *Sadhaka*; and he can make it dance to his tune, control it according to his will, and mould it as he pleases. Mind, the instrument of Satan in man, the magic wand of *Maya*, the terror of all spiritual aspirants, is there in the hands of this music. The wonder of wonders in the case of this music Yoga is that it is that it is not only the mind of the musician which is thus controlled, but the minds of all those who listen to the music. They become calm, peaceful and blissful.

This is why great saints like Mira Bai, Tukaram, Kabir Das, Sri Tyagaraja, Purandara Das and others wove their *upadesas* into sweet music; with the sweet music, these sublime thoughts would easily get into the heart of the listener, which is at other times zealously guarded by the vicious cobra of worldliness.

Many sages affirm that many diseases can be cured by the melodious sound of a flute or a violin, a *Veena* or a *Sarangi*. They maintain that there is, in music, an extraordinary power over diseases. Harmonious rhythm caused by sweet music has attractive property as it draws out diseases. The disease comes out to encounter the music wave and the two blend together and vanish in space.

Music also relaxes nervous tension, and makes parts of the body affected by tension to resume their normal functions. Music as a therapy is being now used very often to treat patients suffering from nervous tension. In ancient Egypt, music was used in temples to heal diseases of the nervous class.

However, *Kirtan* is the best medicine and tonic when all other systems of medicines have failed to cure a disease. *Kirtan*, which is singing of the Lord's glories, should take place at the bedside of the patient although it may not be possible all the time. This form of music is the sole refuge and sheet anchor in the treatment of chronic, incurable diseases. The harmonious vibrations produced by the singing of the Lord's name help devotees to control their mind easily. They produce a benign influence on their minds and elevate it at once from its old ruts to magnanimous heights of divine splendour and glory.

PSYCHOLOGY BEHIND KIRTAN BHAKTI

Kirtan is a very effective method of devotion for another reason. Man is an erotic being. He loves but his love is only passion and not pure divine love. He wants to hear sweet music, wants to see beautiful objects and wants to witness a dance.

Music melts the heart of even a stone-hearted man. If at all there is anything that can change the heart of a man in a short span of time that is music and dance. This very method is made use of in *Kirtan Bhakti*; but it is directed towards God instead of sensual enjoyments.

Man's emotion of eroticism is directed towards Divinity, and his love for music and singing is not destroyed; because, sudden destruction of such a sentiment, which he holds as very dear will not prove successful in making him perfect. *Kirtan* is sweet and pleasant and easily changes heart.

GRECO-ROMAN PHILOSOPHIES ON ANGER

Chapter 10

Greek philosophy is widely accepted as the foundation on which Western philosophy is based. Socrates the great scholar and his student Plato believed that man's purpose in life was to seek *sophia*, or wisdom. Achieving sophia gave man a general understanding of the nature of virtue. And once a man reached an understanding of each of the virtues, he would naturally live them. However, Aristotle, who was Plato's student, believed that virtuous living also required a different kind of wisdom, one that was more particular and practical than the abstract, ethereal, and general wisdom of sophia. Aristotle called this different kind of wisdom *phronesis*.

Phronesis has been translated in different ways, "prudence" being the most common one. But the translation that best suited is "practical wisdom." According to him, practical wisdom is the Master Virtue and a true characteristic that is bound up with action, accompanied by reason, and concerned with things good and bad for a human being.

Both Plato and Aristotle have written about anger in their books extremely lucidly. While explaining the dangers of anger philosophically, they have also commented extensively on the practical wisdom and virtue of overcoming anger.

The Greco-Roman philosophers do not categorise anger as good or bad. They simply state that anger, when used at the right place, at the right time and for a right duration is not bad. According to the Western philosophy, any and every body can get angry, but the trick is how to use anger in a constructive manner and not in a destructive way.

PLATO ON ANGER

Plato was a renowned philosopher, mathematician and an influential figure in Ancient Greece. A student of Socrates, Plato was born around the year 428 BCE in Athens and founded a school of learning which he called the Academy. The institution, which was erected in the Greek capital was the first ever institution of higher learning in the Western world.

Along with Socrates and his most famous student, Aristotle, Plato helped to lay the foundations of Western philosophy and science. Alfred North Whitehead once noted: "The safest general characterization of the European philosophical tradition is that it consists of a series of footnotes to Plato."

The Greco-Roman philosophers do not categorise anger as good or bad. They simply state that anger, when used at the right place, at the right time and for a right duration is not bad. According to the Western philosophy, any and every body can get angry, but the trick is how to use anger in a constructive manner and not in a destructive way.

BOOK: THE REPUBLIC

In his work, 'The Republic', based on the definition of justice, the order and character of the Just city-state and the Just man, Plato says: "It isn't unreasonable for us to claim that they are two, and different from one another. We'll call the part of the soul with which it calculates the rational part and the part with which it lusts, hungers, thirsts and gets excited by other appetites the irrational appetitive part, companion of certain indulgences and pleasures.

Then, let these two parts be distinguished in the soul. Now, is the spirited part by which we get angry a third part or is it of the same nature as either of the other two? Perhaps it's like the appetitive part. It certainly proves that anger sometimes makes war against the appetites, as one thing against another. Besides, don't we often notice in other cases that when appetite forces someone contrary to rational calculation, he reproaches himself and gets angry with that in him that's doing the forcing, so that of the two fractions that are fighting a civil war, so to speak, spirit allies itself with reason? But I don't think you can say that you've ever seen spirit, either in yourself or anyone else, ally itself with an appetite to do what reason has decided must not be done".

BOOK: THE PHILEBUS

In Philebus, one of the surviving Socratic dialogues, written in the 4th century B.C. by Plato, the Greek philosopher mentions a dialogue between a young man called Protarchus and Socrates.

It starts as the following:

Socrates: Take wrath, fear, longing, lamentation, love, jealousy, malice, and other things like that; don't you regard them as a kind of pain within the soul itself?

Protarchus: I certainly do.

Socrates: And don't we find that they are full of marvellous pleasures? Or do we need the famous lines as a reminder about wrath:

.... That can embitter even the wise

.... But much sweeter than soft-flowing honey.... (*Illyad* by Homer)

BOOK: THE LAWS

The Laws, Plato's longest dialogue, has for centuries been recognized as the most comprehensive description of the practical consequences of his philosophy, which was his vision to have an Ideal Republic.

In this particular work, recognizing the disastrous effects of anger and bad language that often goes along with it, the Greek philosopher states:

There are several kind of madness, brought on by several causes. The causes that are the result of illness, but there are some people with an unfortunate natural irritability, made worse by poor discipline, who in any trivial quarrel will shout their heads off in mutual abuse. Such a thing is highly improper in a well-run state. So this single law should apply to all cases of defamation: no one is to defame anybody.

If you are having an argument, you should listen to your opponents' case, and put your own to him and the audience, without making any defamatory remarks at all. When men take to damning

> There are several kind of madness, brought on by several causes. The causes that are the result of illness, but there are some people with an unfortunate natural irritability, made worse by poor discipline, who in any trivial quarrel will shout their heads off in mutual abuse.

and cursing each other and to calling each other rude names in shrill tones, these mere words, empty though they are soon lead to real hatreds and quarrels of the most serious kind.

In satisfying his ugly emotion, anger, and in thus disgracefully stroking the fires of his fury, the speaker drives back into primitive savagery a side of his character that was once civilized by education, and such a bad tempered life makes him no better than a wild animal; bitter indeed, he finds, are the pleasures of anger. Besides on such occasions all men are usually quick to resort to ridicule of their opponents, and no one who has indulged that habit has ever acquired the slightest sense of responsibility or remained faithful to many of his principles. That is why no one must ever breathe a word of ridicule in a temple or at a public sacrifice or at the games or in the marketplace or in court or in any public gathering and the relevant official must always punish such offenses.

ARISTOTLE ON ANGER

> *Anger is a desire, accompanied by pain, for apparent retribution, aroused by an apparent slighting against oneself or those connected to oneself, the slighting being undeserved.*

These are the wise words of renowned Greek philosopher and scientist Aristotle, whose writings has covered many subjects — including physics, biology, zoology, metaphysics, logic, ethics, aesthetics, poetry, theatre, music, rhetoric, linguistics, politics and government — and constitute the first comprehensive system of Western philosophy.

Student of renowned Greek philosopher and mathematician, Plato, Aristotle is credited with tutoring Alexander the Great between 356 and 323 BCE. According to the Encyclopaedia Britannica, "Aristotle was the first genuine scientist in history".

In the Book Ethica Nicomachea, the Greek philosopher says that good temper is a means with respect to anger; the middle state being unnamed, and the extremes almost without a name as well. According to him, people place good temper in the middle position, though it inclines towards the deficiency, which is without a name. The excess might be called a sort of 'irascibility'. For, the passion is anger, while its causes are many and diverse.

According to disposition, there are different types of men:

GOOD-TEMPERED MAN

A man who is angry at the right things, with the right people, at the right time and as long as he ought to be is praised. For a good-tempered man is not revengeful, but rather tends to make allowances.

BAD-TEMPERED MAN

We call bad-tempered those who are angry at the wrong things, more angry than is right, and for longer, and cannot be appeased until they inflict vengeance or punishment.

HOT-TEMPERED MAN

Hot-tempered men often get angry quickly and with the wrong people and at wrong things and more than is right, but their anger

> In satisfying his ugly emotion, anger, and in thus disgracefully stroking the fires of his fury, the speaker drives back into primitive savagery a side of his character that was once civilized by education, and such a bad tempered life makes him no better than a wild animal.
>
> *– Plato*

ceases quickly, which is the best point about them. This happens to them because they do not restrain their anger but retaliate openly, owing to their quickness of temper, and then their anger ceases.

SULKY PEOPLE

People of this nature are hard to appease, and retain their anger long; for they repress their passion. But it ceases when they retaliate; for revenge relieves them of their anger, producing in them pleasure, instead of pain. Such people are most troublesome to themselves and to their dearest friends.

What we have said in our earlier treatment is basically that it is not easy to define how, with whom, at what and how long one should be angry, and at what point right action ceases and wrong begins. Sometimes we praise those who exhibit deficiency, and call them good-tempered, and sometimes we call angry people manly, as being capable of ruling.

It is not a coincidence that in the *Ditiya* (second) *Aghata Pativinaya Sutta* it is mentioned that there are five types of people in this world:

FIRST PERSON

The first type of person is one who has an immoral conduct and always does unethical deeds. However, his tone and words are virtuous. It is easy to remember him as a person with immoral behaviour but virtuous words. Like some politicians who only use delightful words without any action.

SECOND PERSON

Although this person has a moral behaviour, his speech is immoral. Some do not talk politely and scold kindly all the time. Some scold even after donating. Although giving is a noble quality, scolding thereafter saying, "Don't ever sight this place again," is cruel. Although his speech is immoral, his act is moral.

THIRD PERSON

Their conduct and speech are both immoral. Nevertheless, a virtuous thought comes by occasionally.

FOURTH PERSON

Their conduct and speech are both immoral and a virtuous thought does not come by even occasionally.

FIFTH PERSON

All actions, words and thoughts are moral.

MARCUS AURELIUS, EPICTETUS AND SENECA ON ANGER

Marcus Aurelius writes in his Meditation: When you are angry above measure, think within yourself, how momentary man's life is. Let us think how much more grievous are the consequences of our anger than the acts which arouse it. Let this truth be present to you in the excitement of anger, that to be moved by passion is not manly, but that mildness and gentleness, as they are more human, so also are they more manly.

Epictetus says: Whenever you are angry, be assured that it is not only a present evil, but you have also augmented a habit, and added fuel to fire. If you desire not to be of an angry temper, then, do not feed the habit. Give it nothing to help its increase. Be quiet at first, and reckon the days in which you have not been angry. 'I used to be angry every day; now every other day; then every third day or fourth day.' And if you miss being angry for as long as thirty days, offer a grateful thanks-giving to God.

Seneca says: The greatest remedy for anger is delay. When angry, count 10 before you speak, if very angry, count 100. This is the substance of their practical precepts. The idea is to put a brake on anger.

CHINESE AND JAPANESE PHILOSOPHIES ON ANGER

Chapter 11

The Eastern philosophers have a very practical approach towards anger. They believe that a person should only speak when spoken to and before talking one should not only think with a clear mind, but also think about the detrimental consequences of his words.

Another concept that the Eastern philosophers highlight is that one should be aware of what is going on around him or her and be prepared to take action immediately to repair or enhance any situation or relationship in which he or she is involved.
Ways pertaining to divert the mind from getting angry are also mentioned in the Eastern Philosophy.

CONFUCIUS

"When anger rises, think of the consequences" is what Confucius, a highly regarded Chinese teacher, editor, politician, and philosopher cautioned his followers in his teachings compiled in The Analects.

The philosophy of Confucius emphasized personal and governmental morality, correctness of social relationships, justice and sincerity. He bought out the concept of the Superior Man - not in status or wealth but by intellect and virtue.

Born in 551 B.C., in the feudal state of Lu, Confucius was of the opinion that a person who aims to be a complete man of virtue in his food does not seek to gratify his appetite, nor in his dwelling place does he seek the appliances of ease; he is earnest in what he is doing, and careful in his speech; he frequents the company of men of principle that he may be rectified:- such a person may be said indeed to love to learn.

Confucius who was born into the class of Shi, between the aristocracy and the common people and is said to have worked as a shepherd, cowherd, clerk, and a book-keeper, in his teachings also said: "There is the love of knowing without the love of learning; the beclouding here leads to dissipation of mind. There is the love of being sincere without the love of learning; the beclouding here leads to an injurious disregard of consequences. There is the love of straight forwardness without the love of learning; the beclouding here leads to rudeness. There is the love of boldness without the love

> "Respectfulness, without the rules of propriety, becomes laborious bustle; carefulness, without the rule of propriety, becomes timidity; boldness, without the rules of propriety, becomes insubordination; straightforwardness, without the rules of propriety, becomes rudeness".

of learning; the beclouding here leads to insubordination. There is the love of firmness without the love of learning; the beclouding here leads to extravagant conduct".

On the concept of human mind Confucius viewed: "The mind of the superior man is conversant with righteousness; the mind of the mean man is conversant with gain. The superior man wishes to be slow in his speech and earnest in his conduct".

He further said: "The superior man, extensively studying all learning, and keeping himself under the restraint of the rules of propriety, may thus likewise not overstep what is right. The superior man is satisfied and composed; the mean man is always full of distress".

The great Chinese philosopher is also credited for making an attempt to remove the disturbing elements in society. He strained his every nerve in giving moral training to people. He laid emphasis on cultivation of ethical virtues.

According to him: "What is the good of being ready with the tongue? They who encounter men with smartness of speech for the most part procure themselves hatred. I know not whether he be truly virtuous, but why should he show readiness of the tongue?"

While speaking about one of his disciples and his love for learning, Confucius said that Yen Hui was one of his favoured disciples who loved to learn. "Yen Hui loved to learn. He did not transfer his anger; he did not repeat a fault. Unfortunately his appointed time was short and he died; and now there is not such another. I have not yet heard of anyone who loves to learn as he did".

Confucius had a strong conviction that if superiors and elders had a blameless character, others would follow them and there would be love and universal peace everywhere.

The Chinese philosopher said: "Respectfulness, without the rules of propriety, becomes laborious bustle; carefulness, without the rule of propriety, becomes timidity; boldness, without the rules of propriety, becomes insubordination; straightforwardness, without the rules of propriety, becomes rudeness".

He was also of the opinion that there are three principles of conduct which the man of high rank should consider specially important: 1) That in his deportment and manner he should keep from violence and heedlessness; 2) That in regulating his countenance he should keep near to sincerity; and 3) That in his words and tones he should keep far away from lowness and impropriety. As to such matters as attending to the sacrificial vessels, there are the proper officers for them.

Confucius also preached to his disciples: "Though a man has abilities as admirable as those of Duke of Chau, yet if he be proud and niggardly, those other things are really not worth looking at".

BOOK: PERFECT VIRTUE

"The man of perfect virtue is cautious and slow in his speech. The superior man has neither anxiety nor fear".
– Confucius

On Perfect Virtue," the Chinese Master said: "Death and life have their determined appointment; riches and honours depend upon Heaven. Let the superior man never fail reverentially to order his own conduct, and let him be respectful to others and observant of propriety: - then all within the four seas will be his brothers". He

> There are three errors to which they who stand in the presence of a man of virtue and station are liable: *1)* They may speak when it does not come to them to speak - this is called rashness. *2)* They may not speak when it comes to them to speak - this is called concealment. *3)* They may speak without looking at the countenance of their superior - this is called blindness.

further said: "He with whom neither slander that gradually soaks into the mind, nor statements that startle like a wound in the flesh, are successful, may be called intelligent indeed. He, with whom neither soaking slander, nor startling statements are successful, may be calling far-seeing".

According to Confucius, if names not be correct, language is not in accordance with the truth of things. If language be not in accordance with the truth of things, affairs cannot be carried on to success.

He added: "When affairs cannot be carried on to success, proprieties and music do not flourish. When proprieties and music do not flourish, punishments will not be properly awarded. When punishments are not properly awarded, the people do not know how to move hand or foot. Therefore a superior man considers it necessary that the names he uses may be spoken appropriately and also that what he speaks may be carried out appropriately. What the superior man requires is just that in his words there may be nothing incorrect".

The Chinese philosopher was of the opinion that there are three errors to which they who stand in the presence of a man of virtue and station are liable: 1) They may speak when it does not come to them to speak; this is called rashness. 2) They may not speak when it comes to them to speak–this is called concealment. 3) They may speak without looking at the countenance of their superior–this is called blindness.

"The superior man has nine things which are subjects with him of thoughtful consideration: 1) In regard to the use of his eyes, he is anxious to see clearly. 2) In regard to the use of his ears, he is anxious to hear distinctly. 3) In regard to his countenance, he is anxious that it should be benign. 4) In regard to his demeanour, he is anxious that it should be respectful. 5) In regard to his speech, he is anxious that it should be sincere. 6) In regard to his doing of business, he is anxious that it should be reverently careful.7) In regard to what he doubts about, he is anxious to question others. 8) When he is angry, he thinks of the difficulties (his anger may involve him in. 9) When he sees gain to be got, he thinks of righteousness".

Speaking about Perfect Virtue, Confucius said: "To be able to practise five things everywhere under heaven constitutes perfect virtue... (They are) gravity, generosity of soul, sincerity, earnestness, and kindness. If you are grave, you will not be treated with disrespect. If you are generous, you will win all. If you are sincere, people will repose trust in you. If you are earnest, you will accomplish much. If you are kind, this will enable you to employ the services of others. The firm, the enduring, the simple, and the modest are near to virtue".

THE GREAT LEARNING- BOOK OF POETRY

In the Book of Poetry Confucius says: "The point where to rest being known, the object of pursuit is then determined; and, that being determined, a calm unperturbed state may be attained to. To that calmness there will succeed a tranquil repose. In that repose there may be careful deliberation, and that deliberation will be followed by the attainment of the desired end".

He adds: "From the Son of Heaven down to the mass of the people, all must consider the cultivation of the person the root of

> We call bad-tempered those who are angry at the wrong things, more angry than is right, and for longer, and cannot be appeased until they inflict vengeance or punishment.

everything besides. What is meant by, the cultivation of the person depends on rectifying the mind may be thus illustrated: If a man be under the influence of passion he will be incorrect in his conduct. He will be the same, if he is under the influence of terror, or under the influence of fond regard, or under that of sorrow and distress. When the mind is not present, we look and do not see; we hear and do not understand; we eat and do not know the taste of what we eat".

BOOK: THE DOCTRINE OF THE MEAN

"While there are no stirrings of pleasure, anger, sorrow, or joy, the mind may be said to be in the state of Equilibrium. When those feelings have been stirred, and they act in their due degree, there ensues what may be called the state of Harmony. This Equilibrium is the great root from which grow all the human acting in the world, and this Harmony is the universal path, which they all should pursue. Let the states of equilibrium and harmony exist in perfection, and a happy order will prevail throughout heaven and earth, and all things will be nourished and flourish," said Confucius in his Doctrine of the Mean.

Speaking on the issue of energy of the South, energy of the North, or energy, which one should cultivate oneself, Confucius said: "To show forbearance and gentleness in teaching others; and not to revenge unreasonable conduct: this is the energy of southern regions, and the good man makes it his study. To lie under arms; and meet death without regret: this is the energy of northern regions, and the forceful make it their study. Therefore, the superior man cultivates a friendly harmony, without being weak. How firm is he in his energy! He stands erect in the middle, without inclining to either side. How firm is he in his energy! When good principles prevail in the government of his country, he does not change from what he was in retirement. How firm is he in his energy! When bad principles prevail in the country, he maintains his course to death without changing.-How firm is he in his energy!"

LAO TZU ON ANGER

Lao Tzu was a philosopher and poet of ancient China. He is best known as the reputed author of the Tao Te Ching and the founder of philosophical Taoism, but he is also revered as a deity in religious Taoism and traditional Chinese religions.

Although a legendary figure, he is usually dated to around the 6th century BC and reckoned a contemporary of Confucius, but some historians contend that he actually lived during the Warring States period of the 5th or 4th century BC.

A central figure in Chinese culture, Laozi is claimed by both the emperors of the Tang dynasty and modern common folk of the Li family as a founder of their lineage. Throughout history, Lao's work has been embraced by various anti-authoritarian movements.

In his book Tao Te Ching, the Chinese philosopher has compiled some selected commentaries that can prove helpful in not just dealing political issues, but also leading a good and satisfactory life.

Following are a few philosophies of Laozi that have been interpreted by various other scholors. Read on.

The five colors make our eyes blind; the five tones deafen our ears; the five flavors make our mouth numb; riding and hunting make our minds wild; hard to get goods make us commit crimes, thus the rule of the sages; favours the stomach over the eyes thus they pick this over that.

WU CH'ENG interprets this verse as: "Desiring external things harms our bodies. Sages nourish their breath by filling their stomach, not by chasing material objects to please their eyes. Hence, they choose internal reality over external illusion. But the eyes can't help seeing, and the ears can't help hearing, and the mouth can't help tasting, and the mind can't help thinking and the body can't help acting. They can't stay still. But if we let them move without leaving stillness behind, nothing can harm us".

Those who tiptoe don't stand; those who stride don't walk; those who consider themselves don't appear; those who display themselves don't shine; those who flatter themselves achieve nothing; those who parade themselves don't lead. Travelers have a saying: too much food and a tiring pace, some things are simply bad; those who possess the Way thus shun them.

TE-CH'ING interprets this verse as: "People raise themselves up on their tiptoes to see over the heads of others, but they cannot stand like this for long. People take longer strides to stay in front of others, but they cannot walk like this very far. Neither of these is natural".

Those who know others are perceptive; those who know themselves are wise; those who conquer themselves are strong; those who know contentment are wealthy; those who strive hard are resolved; those who don't lose their place endure; those who aren't affected by death live long.

HO-SHANG KUNG interprets this verse as: "If someone can conquer others, it is only by using force. If someone can conquer their own their own desire, no one in the world can compete with them. Hence, we call them strong".

The Tao moves the other way; the Tao works through weakness; the things of this world come from something; something comes from nothing.

LIU CH'EN-WENG interprets this verse as: "Once things reach their limit, they have to go back the other way".

WEI YUAN says: "The Tao moves contrary to how most people look at things".

The weakest thing in the world overcomes the strongest thing in the world; what doesn't exist finds room where their is none thus we know help comes with no effort; wordless instruction; effortless help; few in the world can match this.

YEN TSUN interprets this verse as: "Action is the beginning of chaos. Stillness is the origin of order. Speech is the door of misfortune. Silence is the gate of blessing".

THE SAMURAI CULTURE BY MUSASHI MIYAMOTO

The Samurai culture of Japan is perhaps one of the best ways to understand and practice the concept of Anger Management.

Musashi Miyamoto, the most famous combat strategist in Japanese history was 13 years old when he began his astounding career as a dualist, killing a veteran warrior twice his age. By the time he was 29, he had killed over 60 warriors in death duels. Later on he became a philosopher and recorded his philosophies, strategies in a book Go Rin Sho – The Book of Five Rings. In that book he emphasizes on the following:

UNCLUTTERED MIND

Miyamoto Musashi had no ego at all — a factor that played an extraordinary role in his incredible drive to continue studying and practising swordsmanship all his life and to regard every opponent, no matter how inept, as someone he could learn from.

Zen, the philosophy Musashi followed, teaches that the primary obstacle to enlightenment and wisdom is ego — the selfish and glorified sense of self most people have. Musashi was so ego-less that it drove some of his friends and most of his enemies to distraction — giving him a great advantage over his enemies.

Meditation has long been a cultural custom in Japan, practised by most people at some time or the other, and regularly by priests, tea masters, artists, landscape gardeners, potters, warriors and business people. Some of Japan's most successful businessmen today meditate to enhance their decision making and management skills.

A few Japanese corporations even require all their managers to spend time in temples meditating under the strict supervision of Buddhist priests.

KNOWING YOUR SURROUNDINGS

The 'hidden' message is that you are likely to fail if you do not keep your wits to yourself — a condition as *zanshin* (zahn-sheen), which is translated as "lingering mind".

Many people — most people in fact — are not in a state of *zanshin*, most of their waking hours — meaning that they are kind of coasting mentally; not focused and not being the best that they can be. They just let things slide.

The point is that we should be aware of what is going on around us and be prepared to take action immediately to repair or enhance any situation or relationship in which we are involved.

SIGNIFICANCE OF ART IN LIFE

Despite a lifelong rigorous regime of training his mind and body to kill or defeat his opponents in one-on-one sword fights, Musashi was also the product of a culture that regarded art as essential for the fulfilment of human aspirations, and in the last half of his life he became an artist as well as a warrior.

One of the most important elements in the mindset of Musashi was the existence of a view or belief in the Buddhist concept of *Mushin* (moo-sheen), meaning "no mind" — a state of mind that refers to acting without artifices, without illusions, without being influenced by subjective thinking.

This is the same approach to life followed by many philosophers. Bruce Lee, one of the greatest martial artists of all times, also had *Mushin* view of the world and himself. He said that he had no style, but that he was all style!

Everything that Musashi did was done with the eye and the heart of the consummate artist. He turned *Bushido* (the code of honour and morals developed by the Japanese samurai) into poetry in motion, providing a lesson for all who are desirous of mastering any skill.

The importance of art in human life is taken for granted today, but it is too often forgotten after one finishes elementary school. Thereafter, its practice plays little or no role in the life of the average person.

Another lesson that can be learned from Musashi is that training and practising in a number of arts should continue throughout one's life. One of Musashi's most repeated instructions to his disciples was: "Touch upon all of the arts. Develop a discerning eye in all matters". This idea is still reflected today in Japanese culture.

IMPROVE YOURSELF

One of the basic principles of the training of samurai, particularly in the case of Musashi, was the concept of endeavouring to make yourself better today than you were yesterday, and to repeat this challenge on a daily basis.

This, too, is part of the *kaizen* or continuous improvement mentality that has been a basic part of the Japanese culture from ancient times — a trait that can be traced to the Shinto (a Japanese religion from the early 8th Century and incorporating the worship of ancestors and nature spirits and a belief in sacred power *(kami)* in both animate and inanimate things, spirit of the "eternal now".

The *kaizen* element in Japanese culture is "continuous improvement" and when you retire, like Musashi and other samurai leaders, expect to retire into eternal self-improvement.

There is a tendency in people across the globe to stop trying to improve, after they reach a certain level of skill — and this is one of the reasons why the Japanese have had an advantage in virtually everything they do. They have been culturally conditioned to never stop training.

PRACTICAL WISDOM ON ANGER

Chapter 12

A question can be asked: Can a virtuous person be sinful? That is - Can virtue be right and wrong at the same time?

The truth is, every virtue can easily become a fault if not correctly applied. Frugality can transform into miserliness, chastity can become prudishness, self-reliance can harden into prideful stubbornness, meekness can turn into timidity and even a forgiving person can become egoistical that he is so great! A virtuous person may not even realize that he is slowly sinking into the quicksand of sin like Ravana who became egomaniac when anointed as Lord Siva's foremost disciple. Thus a person must maintain a balance between extremes: that of not applying a virtue enough, and that of applying it too much. For example, courage is the balance between cowardliness and recklessness, loyalty is the balance between fickleness and blind obedience and resolution is the balance between spinelessness and obstinacy.

Of course, striking this balance is easier said than done! This is because the path between the virtues is not always in the same place–it can lie closer to one end of the spectrum or the other, depending on changing circumstances. As we see that many times everything is not white or black but a shade of grey in between. Thus the challenge for the man seeking virtue is to calculate the proper path in a certain situation, and this requires Practical Wisdom. For this reason, Chanakya, Narayana and Sun –Tzu, who were all great political thinkers, believed that practical wisdom was the virtue that made all the other virtues possible. Without the correct application of practical wisdom, the other virtues would be lived too much or too little and turn into vices.

Without the correct application of practical wisdom, the other virtues would be lived too much or too little and turn into vices. Thus a person must maintain a balance between extremes: that of not applying a virtue enough, and that of applying it too much.

The path to happiness is paved with decisions made with practical wisdom. The better your decisions, the more you will progress, the more of your potential you will use, the more your life will flourish. In short, practical wisdom is the path to true happiness and satisfaction.

CHANAKYA ON ANGER

Chanakya was an Indian teacher, philosopher, and royal advisor. Originally a professor of economics and political science at the ancient Takshashila University, Chanakya managed the first Maurya Emperor Chandragupta's rise to power at a young age. He is widely credited for having played an important role in the establishment of the Maurya Empire, which was the first empire in archaeologically recorded history to rule most of the Indian subcontinent. Chanakya served as the chief advisor to both Chandragupta and his son Bindusara. He is the pioneer of Political Realism in India.

Chanakya, traditionally identified as Kautilya or Vishnu Gupta, authored the ancient Indian political treatise called *Arthasastra* (Economics). He is considered as the pioneer in the field of economics and political science in India, and his thoughts are considered as an important precursor to classical economics. His works were lost near the end of the Gupta dynasty and rediscovered in 1905.

FOLLOWING ARE CHANAKYA'S VIEWS ON ANGER:

- Infatuation is the most sickening disease. Greed is the biggest enemy. Anger is the worst fire. And knowledge is the most comforting possession. Infatuation makes the infatuated person lose his mind. He is beyond any reasoning and listens to no one's advice. His mind is diseased with just one obsession, to get the person or thing he desires. In such a state he does something stupid and pays a heavy price. Greed leads to one's downfall. It never does any good just like an enemy. And, like fire, anger does a person great harm. It burns away his relationships with others. Acts done in anger haunt one throughout one's life. Knowledge is the most beneficial of one's assets. The wisdom creates an oasis of peace in one's mind.

- In virtual hell are those who are short-tempered, harsh talkers, quarrelsome, friends with evil people and who serve lowly men. The above-mentioned characters are capable of creating hell for themselves. Those who are short-tempered and bad tongued, will create enemies. In a short period they will find themselves surrounded by enemies. Everyone would be declaring to settle scores with them. A poor man rots in the hell of loneliness because no one would like to be near him. A quarrelsome person is the cousin brother of ill-tempered and harsh-tongued ones. He will also suffer the same fate. And one, who has evil people for friends, is courting disaster. He will be in trouble in a little time.
- Anger is like death. Feeling of revenge is like river of agony. Education provides everything to a man and contentedness is a great blessing. Anger is a raging fire that burns a person's body without sending out flames. Too much greed ultimately drowns one in the river of woes. Education and contentment has already been commented upon.
- One whose anger does not inspire anyone, pleasing whom does not deliver profit, and one without authority to punish or reward are nothing but insignificant. One can command the attention of people if one has some power to influence the fate of others physically or spiritually. A powerless person is like a toothless lion that gradually perishes due to ineffectiveness.
- A real student should refrain himself from love, flattery, anger, infatuations, preening, entertainment, and oversleeping. All other refrains are logical except the one about flattery. It can be implied in two ways. One is that flattery by the fellow students can make one a vain person, which will do no good. The other is

> **A really wise man is one who is aware about the art of speaking, talks as per situation, speaks the words that add to his fame, and shows anger in accordance with the power he possesses.**

that the student who becomes a flatterer harms his studies thus ruining his own career.

The following verses are self-explanatory:

- A man must not become vain upon doing charity, penance, gaining knowledge, cultivating politeness and on becoming worldly wise. Because this world is full of gems who excel in these fields and are far more accomplished. There is always one better.
- O man! If you want to win this world with just one act, then don't let your tongue speak ill of any other person. That is it.
- A really wise man is one who is aware about the art of speaking, talks as per situation, speaks the words that add to his fame, and shows anger in accordance with the power he possesses.
- A polite talker endears himself to everyone. One should speak sweetly. It costs nothing. So why be miserly with sweet words?
- Often it is the helplessness that forces people to act good. A weak person acquires friendly nature due to his inability to oppose the stronger. A poor fellow may position himself on peak-of-morality because he cannot afford to have luxuries and women.

  A sick turns into a highly religious person, and an old lady becomes very virtuous because she can no more act naughty.

HITOPDESHA ON ANGER

Hitopdesha was written by Pandit Narayana in the 14th Century AD in Bengal on the behest of King Dhavalachandra. It is based on *Panchatantra* written by Pt. Vishnu Sarma in approximately 2000 BC in Kashmir. *Panchantrata* forms the basis of *Niti Shastra*. The word *Niti* means wise conduct of life.

Hitopdesa is a collection of Sanskrit fables in prose and verse meant to educate young princes on statecraft. The only clue to the identity of the author of Hitopadesha is found in the concluding verses of the work, which supply the name Narayana and mention the patronage of a king called Dhavalachandra. As no other work by this author is known, and since the ruler mentioned has not been traced in other sources, we know almost nothing of either of them. Dating the work is therefore problematic.

There are quotations within it from 8th century works, but the earliest manuscript dates from 1373. Internal evidence may point to an East Indian origin during the later Pala Empire. In his own introductory verses, Narayana mentions that he is indebted to the *Panchatantra* 'and another work', although the sources turn out to be much more various. The Hitopadesha has the same story frame as the *Panchatantra* and many of the same tales are retold, although ten of them appear to come from elsewhere. Furthermore it differs by having only four divisions to the *Panchatantra's* five. However, the latter furnishes only a third of the verses quoted.

Mentioned below are a few interesting verses from the Hitopdesha that can help people lead a successful life.

- From greed proceeds disquietude, from greed springs up the desire (for pleasures), and from greed results infatuation and (finally) ruins; greed is the root of sin.
- The existence of a gold deer was impossible and yet Rama coveted (such) a deer; as a general rule when (some) calamity is impending the talents of men become clouded.

One should give up the collection of these six, viz., lust, anger, want of judgement, greed, vanity and haughtiness: when these are abandoned a man becomes happy.

- A man wishing for welfare in this world should avoid these six faults: sleepiness, slothfulness, timidity, anger, idleness and dilatoriness.
- No one is anybody's friend or anybody's foe: it is the behaviour (or, intercourse) that makes friends of foes.
- The mind of a good man, although made to fly into a great passion, is not affected (by anger); it is not possible to beat the water of the sea with a torch of straw.
- The union of metals is due to their flexibility, of beasts and birds to some cause, of fools to fear or (the prospect of gain), while of good men to (mere) sight.
- Judgement is led astray (warped) by (avarice); avarice begets desire; and a man troubled by desire meets with misery both here and hereafter.
- Even after studying the *Shastras* people remain fools; that man is learned who puts his knowledge into practice: a medicine, although well selected, does not restore the diseased to health by the mere mention of its name.
- The knowledge of theory does not do the least good to one, who shrinks from a determined exertion (perseverance): does a lamp, in this world, reveal a thing to a blind man although it be placed on the palm of his hand?
- He is a wise man who knows how to address a speech suited to an occasion or to act in a manner befitting one's good intention or to be angry in proportion to one's strength.
- Mental agitation is the first (greatest) obstacle to success of

every kind: does not water, even though exceedingly cold, break through a mountain?

- A drunkard, one exceedingly careless, one gone mad (or, who is delirious), one fatigued, one who is in the power of anger, one who is hungry; one who is covetous, one who is timid, one engaged in a business brooking no delay, and, a lover, mind not what is just.
- Pain is the real thing (existing in the world), and not happiness, since that is observed; the term happiness is applied to the removal (of the pain) of one afflicted with sorrow.
- The soul is a river which has self-restraint for its holy stairs, truthfulness for its water, good disposition for its banks and mercy for its waves; bathe in the river, O son of Pandu: the inner soul is not purified by (physical) water.
- Association (with other persons) should be given up by all means; if it cannot be given up it should be made with the good; for the company of the good is a medicine (for the disease of attachment to worldly things).
- Desire should be abandoned by every effort, if it cannot be abandoned, it should be entertained with respect to final emancipation; for such a desire is the medicine for (removing) it (desire in general).

One should give up the collection of these six, viz., lust, anger, want of judgement, greed, vanity and haughtiness: when these are abandoned a man becomes happy.

THIRUKKURAL ON ANGER

Thirukkural is a classic Tamil sangam literature comprising of 1330 couplets or *Kurals*. It was authored by Thiruvalluvar, a poet who is said to have lived anytime between 2nd and 5th century BCE.

> One's expression of anger is dangerous to oneself in places, where that anger is directed against persons stronger than one. But nothing is more evil, when that anger is directed against those who are weaker than one.

The Thirukkural is one of the most important works in the Tamil language. This is reflected in some of the other names by which the text is given by such as Tamil marai (Tamil Vedas); Poyyamozhi (words that never fail); and Deiva nool (divine text). The book is considered to precede Manimekalai and Silapathikaram since they both acknowledge the *Kural* text.

Thirukkural is structured into 133 chapters, each containing 10 couplets, for a total of 1330 couplets. The 133 chapters are grouped into three sections: righteousness, wealth and love.

According to this universal Tamil scripture, the entity of anger is latent in every person. But it shall not be allowed to surface. Anger arises in a person mainly when his faults are pointed out to him.

Following are a few couplets that should help you understand the issues surrounding anger better.

- One's expression of anger is dangerous to oneself in places, where that anger is directed against persons stronger than one. But nothing is more evil, when that anger is directed against those who are weaker than one.
- If a person wants to safeguard himself against all miseries, his anger should be controlled lest that anger should bring about several harsh sufferings leading to his ultimate destruction.
- The fire of anger kills not only the person in whom it resides, but also his kith and kin, who act as good philosophers and guide to him to cross the sea of birth to attain salvation.
- Uttering useless and unfriendly words without any decorum or

culture will show that the speaker of such words is bereft of a sense of justice and this keeps him away from good qualities.

- Speak only the choicest of words of value and avoid speaking words that are not so.
- If a man, while seeking to speak usefully, speaks also sweetly, his sins will diminish and his virtue will increase.
- Let self-control be guarded as a treasure; there is no greater source of good for man than that.
- Knowing that self-control is knowledge, if a man should control himself, in the prescribed course, such self-control will bring him distinction among the wise.
- If a man's speech be productive of a single evil, all the good by him will be turned into evil.

ON UTTERENCE OF PLEASANT WORDS

Pleasant words are words with all pervading love that burn; Words from his guileless mouth who can the very truth discern.

- Sweet words are those which imbued with love and free from deceit flow from the mouth of the virtuous.

With brightly beaming smile, and kindly light of loving eye; And heart sincere, to utter pleasant words is charity.

- Sweet speech, flowing from the heart (uttered) with a cheerful countenance and a sweet look, is true virtue.

Humility with pleasant speech to man on earth; Is choice adornment; all besides is nothing worth.

- Humility and sweetness of speech are the ornaments of man; all others are not (ornaments).

The words of sterling sense, to rule of right that strict adhere; To virtuous action prompting, blessings yield in every sphere.

- That speech which, while imparting benefits ceases not to please, will yield righteousness (for this world) and merit (for the next world).

'Tis virtue when, his footsteps sliding not through envy, wrath, lust, evil speech-these four, man onwards moves in ordered path.

- That conduct is virtue which is free from these four things: malice, desire, anger and bitter speech.

SUN TZU ON ANGER

Traditionally credited as the author of The Art of War, Sun Tzu, a Chinese military general, strategist and philosopher wrote an extremely influential ancient Chinese book on military strategy. Tzu has had a significant impact on Chinese and Asian history and culture, both as the author of The Art of War and as a legendary historical figure.

In his book Tzu says that personal success arises from who you really are. This self- reality, according to him, transcends the events in our life.

In the sub-section of chapter titled: 'Attack by Fire: Be Disruptive and Intrusive': 'Exercise Restraint', Tzu says that a sovereign should not launch a war simply out of anger, nor should a general fight a war simply out of resentment. Take action if it is to your advantage; cancel the action if it is not. An angered man can be happy again, just as a resentful one can feel pleased again, but a state that has perished can never revive, nor can a dead man be brought back to life.

According to Sun Tzu, flexibility is critical for a good general because "as water has no constant form there are in war no constant conditions". Later on, he says "Of the five elements, none is always predominant; of the four seasons, none is permanent; of the days some are long some short and the moon waxes and wanes." Anger robs you of flexibility by making your attitude rigid.

PRINCIPLES AND PRACTICES OF PSYCHOLOGY ON ANGER

Chapter 13

Research on anger started in earnest following the discovery of linkages between mismanaged anger-hostility and serious physical health problems, such as high blood pressure, heart attack and stroke (Helmers, *Poluszny & Krantz 1994*). In people with heart problems, anger outbursts are more likely to precede heart attack than any other type of triggering factors. Poorly regulated anger is also an important element of many mental disorders, and, when coupled with impulsivity, is known to increase suicide risk.

Not only physically, anger has also been associated with many serious negative mental consequences, such as aggressive behaviour *(Cornell, Peterson, & Richards, 1999; Deffenbacher, Oetting, Lynch, & Morris, 1996)*, family violence *(Jacobson et al, 1994; Whiteman, Fanshel, & Grundy, 1987)* and substance abuse *(PeMoja & Spielberger, 1997; Wallfish, Massey, & Krone, 1990)*. Because anger is both common and debilitating, it is important that psychology develops, studies, and disseminates effective interventions to practitioners.

There is sufficient evidence that men are more likely than women to exhibit the cynical type of hostility and/or intense, poorly controlled anger that has been linked to hypertension, heart disease, and premature death and there is a need to compare and contrast men's anger narratives with themes of anger experience that were noted in previous studies of women over the past decade, thereby, contributing to the literature on gender differences in social experiences.

SOCIAL CONCEPT OF MASCULINITY

There is considerable evidence that traditional gender role socialization for masculinity, or, so called, manliness in various cultures discourages boys' feelings of sadness and vulnerability, but promotes aggressive acts, when anger is aroused. This "manliness" ideology develops as growing boys internalize cultural norms and expectations about gender-appropriate behaviour.

Studies show that fathers begin to stimulate their sons to aggressive action from ages as young as 1.5-2 years; by age 3, boys wrestle, kick, push, shove, and hit more often than girls do. Observational studies show that preschool-aged children prefer sex-segregated play. The play of boys often involves struggles for dominance in rough-and-tumble games.

In a study of 3 to 6-year-olds, Martin and Fabes (2001) found a

> Traditional gender role socialization for masculinity, or, so called, manliness in various cultures discourages boys' feelings of sadness and vulnerability, but promotes aggressive acts, when anger is aroused. Fathers begin to stimulate their sons to aggressive action from ages as young as 1.5-2 years; by age 3, boys wrestle, kick, push, shove, and hit more often than girls do.

"social dosage effect", that is, the greater the amount of time spent in play with same-sex peers, the greater the display of stereotypical gender-typed behaviour. Research showed that boys' patterns of aggressive behaviour are already taking shape by the age of eight. According to the boy code, boys must exhibit toughness and deny fear and weakness.

As adults, individuals could choose not to conform to gender stereotypes, but ongoing forces within the social environments of adult men may tend to keep them within the narrow masculine gender roles inculcated, while growing up. It is widely believed that men consider anger acceptable, particularly when expressed in physical aggression.

WHY DO MEN GET ANGRY?

THEME 1: RIGHT VERSUS WRONG

Anger was deeply connected to the men's views of right and wrong. Abstract principles and standards about proper human conduct (e.g. truth, fairness, sportsmanship, and professionalism) were often invoked to explain their angry feelings. Men use terms such as "legitimate", "rational", and "justified" to describe this anger.

"Justified" anger was expressed about a variety of societal issues ranging from the specific (e.g. so and so not doing the "right thing") to the global (e.g. politics, monopolies, environmental pollution, and misuse of some system). Judgements were made that other people should not be inconsistent, irresponsible, incompetent, or manipulative. Men in this category longed to accomplish resolution of perceived wrongs against themselves or others in two manners:

RIGHT AND WRONG ANGER

Anger, if "funnelled and channelled properly" could be used as an instructional device to "drive a point home". "Right anger" was proportionate to the offense and successful in making its point: "You are going to work for justice and people are going to know what your point is, but you're not going to yell at them".

Wrong anger could involve failure to act as well as overreaction. Most shameful is the failure to act, according to internalized norms of masculinity. A number of men doubt their own ability to fulfil societal expectations and question whether they are "adequate" or "normal".

THEME 2: BEING CONTROLLED VERSUS HAVING AND MAINTAINING CONTROL

According to a study, men became angry when they did not have the ability to control or "fix" things, whether the things were inanimate objects (computers, cars) or work-related problems (demanding customers, incompetent co-workers).

Illogical actions of other people that were out of the men's sphere of personal control also provoked considerable ire, consistent with an implicit "should" that human action should be logical and reasonable. In many studies, men often expressed doubt that the emotion of anger could be brought under volitional control. Anger was depicted as an "it", a separate entity that could immobilize or compel rash actions.

> Anger, if "funnelled and channelled properly" could be used as an instructional device to "drive a point home".

Having control, and maintaining control, was viewed as desirable but difficult (or impossible) to achieve. The initial attempt to gain control usually involved "fixing" the machine that was malfunctioning or bringing other people into compliance through some sort of disciplinary measures.

When this initial attempt was unsuccessful withdrawal was a common tactic. The anger had to be "shut down", "leashed", or "bridled" by disengaging from the interaction and isolating oneself.

THEN AND NOW

Most men, according to a study, drew sharp contrasts between their anger then and now. Youthful volatility was contrasted with a more reflective and mature adult anger style.

Some men spoke of a particular event in which they became acutely aware of their capability to kill, after which they relinquished physical fighting as a means of settling disputes. Several other participants attributed a radical change in their anger behaviour to a spiritual or religious transformation. That higher sense of morality involved empathy. All participants describe anger as a problematic uncomfortable emotion. It's dangerous, destructive potential was emphasized more so than its potential to rectify wrongs.

Studies demonstrate several commonalities between the anger experiences of men and women. Findings suggest that men are often as uncomfortable and conflicted about anger as women are. Like women in a previous study *(Thomas et al, 1998),* men often told their anger stories with embarrassed hesitance and nervous laughter. Guilt and self-recrimination regarding anger behaviour were frequently reported by men as well as women. Both men and women were aware of constructive uses of anger, but examples of its constructive use were outnumbered by incidents in which it had caused others pain. Individuals of both genders lacked skill in effective anger management and endorsed the widely held folk concept that anger is an independent entity that takes control of the body and compels unwanted behaviour *(Lakoff, 1987).*

WOMEN'S ANGER AND AGGRESSION

SOCIAL CONCEPT OF FEMININITY

Gender role socialization plays a tremendous part in modelling a woman's personality. Its idea for femininity instils the ideal of the self-less, ever-nurturing "perfect mother" *(Bernardez, 1987)* whose task is to help, comfort, agree, comply, understand, and promote relationship harmony. Women's anger is dangerous because it upsets the status quo *(Miller, 1983)*. Expressing it forthrightly results in derogatory labels such as bitch, shrew, nag, scold, or castrator *(Lerner, 1985).* Women learn these lessons well, stifling their anger much of the time to avert negative consequences.

Recorded in an interview was: "We women want peace more than we want to actually express our anger and have somebody to deal with it. Because then we have to deal with it too. It's a lot easier just to suppress it and not make anybody unhappy. And not have to deal with a confrontation, which bothers me". *(Thomas, Smucker & Droppleman, 1998, p.312)*

Because anger is a normal human emotion, aroused by frequently occurring violations of women's values, beliefs, or rights, where does it go if women habitually suppress it? Many studies show that much of it is confined within the body, where it is an "undercurrent, day after day" *(Thomas et al, 1998).* Women used cooking metaphors to describe the internal agitation: Anger was "simmering", "stewing",

> Various studies have revealed that most pervasive theme of women's anger was powerlessness. Women wanted someone or something to change and they could not make that happen. Not being listened to is perhaps the epitome of powerlessness. Anger was directed at the self when a woman felt she lacked energy or competence to accomplish all that she expected of herself.

and sometimes coming to a "slow boil". Holding the anger inside sometimes requires considerable effort. Women admitted using the passive-aggressive behaviours they had learned from their mothers.

THE TRIGGERING EFFECTS

Various studies have revealed that most pervasive theme of women's anger was powerlessness. Women wanted someone or something to change and they could not make that happen. In fact, it was not uncommon for a woman to say that her significant others or co-workers were not even listening to her views or requests. Not being listened to is perhaps the epitome of powerlessness. Anger was directed at the self when a woman felt she lacked energy or competence to accomplish all that she expected of herself.

A second theme, injustice, included accounts of unfair or disrespectful treatment and betrayal of trust (e.g. son lying, co-worker blaming for a mistake on the job, condescending sexist behaviour). Irresponsibility of family, friends, and co-workers — behaviour that was incongruent with the women's ideologies of commitment and responsibility.

A frequent trigger of women's anger was the failure of husbands and children to do their fair share of household chores. In fact, family members were the most frequently cited triggers of women's anger, although women reported unwillingness to discuss their anger with these same family members. Rather than expressing it, which might clear the air and produce solutions to their grievances, women often ruminated, rehashing the injustices, which generated further resentment.

Considerable anger also was generated by indirect stress. Many studies indicate that women's Number One stressors actually are events or problems occurring in the lives of their circle of their near and dear ones. These stresses become a woman's stress too, because of her connectedness to these loved ones. She shoulders their burdens in addition to her own work stress and other personal issues. Moreover what is particularly distressing is that the woman herself has no control over these events occurring in the lives of others. Equally problematic is the potential for serious, long-term, consequences of these indirect stressors. It seems likely that chronic indirect stress will continue to fuel a chronic, impotent kind of anger.

There is a lot of variation among women, with regard to their tendency to become angry and their use of various modes of anger expression. All women are not the same and thus it would be extremely incorrect to regard them as a monolithic group. Some women are inhibited by the lessons they learned in girl hood about femininity, while others no longer believe in these gender-role restrictions. There are women scoring quite high in "trait anger" (a personality tendency to be readily anger prone). These individuals perceive a wider range of stimuli as frustrating or irritating *(Spielberger, 1991)* and tend to express their anger outwardly in a blaming, attacking way, although they sometimes suppress it because of situational constraints. Women scoring high on trait anger cannot easily let go of their anger, keep thinking about what happened all the time and report numerous somatic symptoms of anger like headache, fatigue etc. – the list is endless. Higher "trait anger" is positively correlated with faulty perceptions (e.g. "they are deliberately provoking me"), higher perceived stress, insufficient social support, depression, and lower self-esteem and perceived health status.

Women higher in self-esteem report fewer tendencies to become angry, less rumination over anger-producing events, less somatic anger symptoms, and greater likelihood of discussing their anger rationally in a health-promoting, problem-solving way.

COMMON MYTHS BUSTED

Studies have negated several societal myths.

One: It is commonly presumed that women do not know when they are angry – Wrong, they do know.

Second: Women's anger is always pathological – Wrong, data has revealed constructive uses of anger, although these were not as frequently reported as episodes that produced embarrassment or shame. Stories of women's anger experiences paint a rather disturbing picture, because the stories are filled with pain.

Third: Some experts claim *(e.g. Ellis, 1962)* that anger is an irrational emotion – Wrong, much of women's anger appears to be soundly based in reality, legitimate, and justifiable. It is squarely grounded in interpersonal interactions in which other people deny women power or resources, treat them unjustly, or behave irresponsibly toward them. The offenders are not strangers; rather, they are their closest intimates. Therefore, anger and hurt are often intertwined. Although discussions of anger from Aristotle to Lazarus *(1991)* have emphasized an angry person's desire for revenge, that is not what women say they want. What do women want? The answer is in most studies quite similar: Relational Reciprocity – Women feel that is not unreasonable to expect to be listened to and treated with respect. It is not unreasonable to ask for equitable division of household or workplace labour.

Regardless of culture or geographic location, the most difficult arena for effective anger expression appears to be intimate relationships with men. Even women who were assertive at work and with friends often were reluctant to express anger to their male partners, for fear of "breaking the circle". Irrespective of colour, race, geographical location, women generally occupy subordinate status in patriarchal societies that reserve power for men. Patriarchal societies are by far in the majority across the globe *(Hyde, 2004).*

Anger displays of people with high-status (whether male or female) are judged more appropriate than anger of low- or moderate social status individuals *(Maybury, 1997).* Women's assertiveness rises as their social status rises *(Twenge, 2001).* Thomas (1993) found differences in anger expression when women were categorized according to years of education (i.e., more suppression, more somatic anger symptoms among the less educated). Differences also were found when women were categorized according to the amount of prestige, autonomy, and control conferred by their occupation. Not surprisingly, women relegated by society to the "low prestige" category (homemakers, clerical workers) were more likely to suppress their anger.

Having a good female role model can be very beneficial as seen in studies where women who demonstrated healthy, constructive uses of anger had one while they were growing up. What they learned from their mothers was the gender role imperative to nurture others, a mandate that takes precedence over voicing one's own needs.

Research has shown that mothers generally avoid talking about anger with their daughters. Some women were taught that anger was sinful as well as unfeminine and unattractive. Yet it is clear from many studies that the continual use of restraint, repression, and rumination prevents the resolution of interpersonal conflicts. Unresolved conflicts with significant others fester, therefore, much like a pimple that ultimately becomes a boil. Recent research shows that passive coping (i.e., escape, avoidance) actually leads to

Women higher in self-esteem report fewer tendencies to become angry, less rumination over anger-producing events, less somatic anger symptoms, and greater likelihood of discussing their anger rationally in a health-promoting, problem-solving way.

increased hostility and depressive symptoms, while active coping may have the opposite effect *(Mao, Bardwell, Major & Dimsdale, 2003).*

Thomas and colleagues (1998) recommend training in assertiveness and conflict resolution for women who are unable to use their anger effectively. Cognitive restructuring interventions may need to focus on increasing a woman's self-esteem: She must believe that she is a person of worth before she can request respectful treatment from those who take advantage of her. Righteous anger energizes social action to protect the deprived and self-protective action when one's own rights are violated. Women experiencing high levels of indirect stress, or other chronic stressors, must be taught techniques for regularly discharging negative emotionality, either through vigorous physical activities (jogging, yoga *asanas*) or through calming procedures (meditation, music, relaxation). Women whose anger is too frequent, intense, or prolonged should seek counselling to unravel their "big ball of anger" with a sympathetic and skilled listener. A therapist will foster women's empowerment and ability to make the life changes they desire, "to be free *for* our anger, rather than to be free *from* it". *(Schrader, 1973).*

Actively trying to stifle anger requires effort and eventually takes a toll on both body and psyche. At the very least, women should be encouraged to discuss their anger regularly with a confidant, a practice shown to have benefits with regard to lower blood pressure, lower body mass index, better general health, and greater self-efficacy and optimism. Discussing anger provides women with empathy and support, while releasing ruminative thoughts about the anger-producing event.

WHY DO WOMEN GET ANGRY?

- **Anger Confusing Mixture of Feelings**
  Anger is a confusing and uncomfortable emotion for women. When asked to talk about anger, women often talked about the anger being inextricable from hurt, sadness, disillusionment, disappointment, and other painful feelings.
- **Anger a Violation of Core Values**
  Core values and principles are violated when women are treated unfairly or disrespectfully. They felt that their families should adhere to an implicit relational contract, in which caring and concern are reciprocated. Instead, too often they felt that the situation was one-sided. They resented the multiple and seemingly incessant demands from their husbands, children, in-laws, extended kin, neighbours, and friends. Women spoke of feeling walked on, stretched too thin, and being pulled in too many directions.
- **Powerlessness**
  All study participants described a sense of powerlessness when they did not express anger but confined it within the body. They felt “small”, “diminished”, and “virtually extinguished”. Paradoxically, however, having a volcanic outburst of anger was not the remedy. Overt anger usually emerged after a build-up of stored anger reached a kind of critical mass.

The after-effects of such explosions were usually disastrous. Significant others “blew off” the temporary craziness of the woman’s behaviour, failing to take her legitimate concerns seriously because they were expressed in such a hysterical manner. Not only was the objectionable behaviour of the other person unchanged, the study participants also felt compelled to "take back" their out-of-control anger by profuse apologies and self-recrimination. Their resolve to preserve family harmony often intensified.

MEN'S ANGER VS. WOMEN'S ANGER

Gender differences thus have been observed as well. Whereas women's anger was provoked mainly by lack of relationship reciprocity in their closest intimate relationships, men's anger was often provoked by strangers, faulty mechanical objects, or global/local societal issues in which a principle was at stake or an injustice was perceived.

Expression of anger was distressful to women because it broke the circle of an intimate relationship and created fear of its termination. Women frequently used the word "hurt" and had difficulty separating their anger from feelings of "hurt", but very few of the men ever used the word. Women reported that crying was common while angry; men did not.

ANGRY YOUTH

Out-of-control anger behaviour appears to be rampant among youth, perhaps echoing the behaviour modelled by adults who engage in road rage, air rage, and desk rage. The high frequency of bullying behaviour has been documented in several studies.

Teasing and bullying escalated when students were highly sensitive, cried, or acted "odd". The by-standing audience often supports bullying behaviour; 10% to 20% experienced a vicarious thrill from watching other students being bullied.

A very new phenomenon is, rising violence among girls and young women. They do not get along well with their families; dislike school; have generalized and intense anger, loneliness, and sadness; and may act aggressively when experiencing loneliness and sadness. Some of these girls fit the symptom picture of conduct disorder, or a personality disorder. Other girls may engage in aggressive behavior to create a "wall of self-protection" in an increasingly violent world, a fierce persona that conveys, "Better not mess with me" *(Jack, 1999, p. 85)*. Exposed to a steady diet of violent television and movies and lacking more effective role models, both boys and girls need to learn how to manage dysphoric emotion and interpersonal conflicts without engaging in aggression.

There is no doubt that generational changes are becoming evident. Young women are less inhibited about venting anger outwardly than their mothers and grandmothers. If this change can be attributed to healthy feminist identity development, then it is most encouraging. If females are simply adopting the less desirable aspects of aggressive masculinity, the change will not promote better physical and mental health—nor will it bode well for a better world in which interpersonal conflicts could be brought to the table and settled with rational discussion, negotiation, and compromise.

RISK FACTORS FOR YOUTH VIOLENCE

While the ethology of youth violence is complex, many risk factors are well-known, including family factors such as parental criminality, child maltreatment, and low levels of parental involvement. The predictive power of factors such as poverty, residence in a violent community, and neighbourhood disorganization is also well established.

Researchers have found a direct relationship between school disconnectedness and outcomes such as delinquency, truancy, drug use, and a number of physical and mental health indicators. Students who feel close to others, fairly treated, and vested in school are less likely to engage in risky behaviours than those who do not.

Harsh disciplinary policies (e.g. expulsion for a first offense)

> While the reasons of youth violence are complex, many risk factors are well-known, including family factors such as parental criminality, child maltreatment, and low levels of parental involvement. The power of factors such as poverty, residence in a violent community, and neighbourhood disorganization is also well established.

produce lower school connectedness. Greater connectedness is promoted by a climate of positive classroom management, smaller school size, and higher student participation in extra-curricular activities. This line of research is important because school connectedness is a modifiable factor: Poverty, community disorganisation, and family neglect are not.

ANGER RELATED FACTORS IN YOUTH

Although anger seems to be a response to something outside of us (various objects and events), many times it is an intrapersonal event. Following are the factors responsible for anger-related behaviour:

- **Genetic factor:** Some children are born irritable, touchy and easily angered, and these signs are present from an early age.
- **Socio-cultural factors:** The agents of socialisation often regard anger as negative, and discourage its expression. As a result, we do not learn how to handle it or channel it constructively.
- **Family background:** Often the easily angered come from families that are disruptive, chaotic, and not skilled at emotional communication. Gender differences in aggression/anger remain a human universal with men as more aggressive/anger-prone than women.
- **Self-angering philosophy:** We also generate our own anger philosophically by consciously or unconsciously subscribing to

absolutistic, command-oriented thinking. The underlying cause of many anger related feeling is our self-angering philosophy of "Shoulding" and "Musting". The very irrational expectation that others Should or Must always act fairly, and Should or Must never do otherwise in every situation makes us angry.

COPING WITH ANGER: SILENCE OR EXPLOSION?

A frequently asked question is: Is it good to let all anger out?

Psychologists now say that this is a dangerous myth. Some people use this theory as a license to hurt others. Recent research shows that such an effort actually escalates anger, and does nothing to help us resolve the situation. Most alarmingly, discharged anger escalates health risk for high BP, heart problems, and even for brain strokes. Unfortunately, people who suppress rage experience the same physical response as those who express their anger/hostility.

Uncontrolled anger wastes energy, affects our judgement, increases tension and leaves us fatigued. One of the most harmful effects of anger is that it robs us of our reason and good sense. No wonder that an angry person is soon avoided by everyone who knows him. Blowing off-steam to get rid of pent up feelings/fury hurts others. However, unexpressed anger/rage (i.e. suppressed) can do us far more harm than candidly and freely expressed feelings. Suppressing anger in all probability leaves us much worse. It can also lead to a pathological change in personality that may seem perpetually cynical and hostile. Many people who are constantly putting others down, criticizing everything and making sarcastic comments are probably suffering from this problem. This happens because they have not learnt how to constructively express their anger. Naturally calming and controlling anger is thus the healthier choice. Even though in real life no one mode may be able to cope up with all the situations, we must make all effort to understand it and control it.

WHEN DO YOU REQUIRE ANGER MANAGEMENT?

ASK YOUR ANGER-O-METER

When is anger management indicated? Most experts agree anger is a problem when it is too frequent, too intense, too prolonged, or managed ineffectively. But the biggest problem is THERE IS YET NO UNIVERSALLY ACCEPTED SCIENTIFIC DEFINITION OF ANGER!

Most psychologists have some sort of a questionnaire to assess a patient, but if you are honest about yourself, the answers to the questions below will tell you exactly what you are in for. So just sit back, relax and answer them truthfully.

- What is your usual proneness to respond angrily (hot-headed vs. slow to respond)?
- How intense is the angry emotionality?
- What is the duration of a typical anger episode? Minutes, hours, days?
- How do you usually express anger? Is it suppressed or directed outward in physical actions or verbal behaviour? How do you feel about your style of anger expression? What are some of its consequences?
- Do you constantly think about the grievance, rekindling anger again and again?
- Are there irrational beliefs fuelling the anger (beliefs about the way other people should behave or about the way a fair world ought to operate)?
- If the anger is kept within, what barriers prevent its expression?
- If the anger is directed outward, do you make a clear, forthright declaration of the anger to the person who provoked it?
- Do you engage in yelling, screaming threats or profanity when angry?
- What triggers the anger? What is it about? What are the recurrent themes, patterns?

- What strategies are used to control temper and cool down? Humour? Meditation? Physical exercise?
- To what degree is anger creating problems for you in the workplace or intimate relationships? Have you ever harmed self or others when angry?
- What defence mechanisms come into play? Intellectualization, denial, projection, isolation?
- How does your current angry behaviour compare to your usual pattern?
- What did you learn about anger while growing up? Do you feel now that it is appropriate?
- Is anger somatised in headaches, gastric distress, or other physical symptoms?
- Is the discomfort of anger medicated through alcohol, drugs, or cigarettes, or food binges?
- With whom does anger most frequently occur? Are there any commonalities among the provocateurs? Do you blame someone else for it?
- In a situation of recurrent conflict, what would you like to be different? Is it possible for you to understand the other person's position on the issue?
- Who will support your efforts to try new anger behaviours? Who may attempt sabotage? How will you respond to saboteurs?

BASIC PRINCIPLES OF ANGER MANAGEMENT: **PSYCHOLOGICAL THERAPY**

Psycho-educational interventions such as Anger Management (AM) are not therapy; the leader functions as teacher and coach, not as therapist. These interventions create the potential for behaviour change by increasing knowledge, providing a new perspective, and giving opportunities to learn and practise specific strategies.

AM training is delivered customarily to groups, because anger is such an interpersonal emotion *(Ander-son-Malico, 1994; Wilson, Davidson, & Reneau, 2000)*. But group therapy has its own drawbacks and individual therapies are being increasingly used as many people are hesitant in front of strangers. Initial interview should be conducted in a one-to-one setting.

There is also a difference in the cause and effect of anger in both men and women. The concerns of midlife people often are quite different from those in their 20s. People who work in the home have a different set of daily frustrations from those who work in a corporate environment.

Research is scant on the anger experience of other ethnic/racial groups, but it is clear, nonetheless, that AM must be tailored sensitively to the age, gender, role responsibilities, developmental level, race, culture of the group members and each individual.

There are various therapies which have been used over a period of time to treat anger, hostility, self-esteem, positive behaviour, relationship, attitude, high blood pressure, etc. They are many but thc most common are: 1. Self-instructional Training, 2. Group Process, 3. Cognitive Restructuring, 4. Problem Solving, 5. Relaxation, 6. Systemic Desensitization, 7. Exposure, Behavioural Skills, 8. Anger Management Training, 9. Education, 10. Meditation, 11. Biofeedback alone and 12. Combination .

ANGER TREATMENT FOR ADULTS: REVIEW OF SCIENTIFIC LITERATURE

Because of the recent proliferation of anger treatment groups, a growing concern has emerged that many "real world programmes" fail to use empirically supported interventions and may have little or no therapeutic or lasting impact on clients (Koerner, 1999). Questions remain about whether or not anger treatment works and what interventions are most likely to be effective.

Practitioners working in different settings may encounter

different types of angry clients. Perhaps this variability has led to a lack of agreement about which anger characteristics are most relevant.

Tafrate (1995) identified 17 published studies and found empirical support for cognitive, relaxation-based, skills training, and multi-component interventions.

Because no agreed-upon diagnostic criteria exist for anger disorders, and because no consensus has yet emerged on what constitutes disturbed anger, anger was not defined as disorder a priory. Future anger research will focus on specific sub-types of anger problems and show that interventions designed to treat sub-types will yield more effective interventions than the present "one size fits all" approach to anger treatment.

THE BIG QUESTION: **DO ANGER MANAGEMENT THERAPIES WORK?**

Results from 50 between-group (treatment vs. no-treatment control) studies indicated that subjects who received treatment were better off than 76% of control subjects. Results from 7 within-group (pre- to post-test single-group designs) studies indicated that 83% of the subjects improved in comparison to their pre-test scores.

This result supports the idea that anger interventions are specific to the constructs of anger, aggression, and hostility and do not appear to work just because of a generalised improvement in negative effect, mental disturbance, or positive well-being.

Anger treatments produced moderate to large improvements on anger self-reports, measures of aggressive behaviours, measures of positive non-angry behaviours, attitudes and cognitions, type A behaviours, and physiological measures.

It appears that anger management interventions produce not just a reduction in the negative effect of anger, but also an equally

> Results from 50 between-group (treatment vs. no-treatment control) studies indicated that subjects who received treatment were better off than 76% of control subjects. Results from 7 within-group (pre- to post-test single-group designs) studies indicated that 83% of the subjects improved in comparison to their pre-test scores.

high effect in increasing positive behaviours.

Aggression had the highest effect size of any type of dependent measure. The fact that anger management programmes result in substantial improvement in aggressive behaviour still does not clarify the relationship between anger and aggression.

Although some generalisation appears to occur, anger treatment has less impact on symptoms of anxiety and depression than on anger or aggression. Another variable that did not appear to improve from anger treatment was self-esteem. This may have occurred because self-esteem deficits may not occur in angry clients. Baumeister (1997) has proposed that angry and aggressive clients harbour high unstable self-esteem and are thus predisposed to respond with anger when confronted with unflattering evaluations from the outside world.

Studies have failed to find a significant difference between types of treatments for different dependent measures. This may have occurred for several reasons. Many interventions have been used. First, little agreement exists among researchers or clinicians as to what constitutes an anger problem. Most studies in this analysis defined anger problems psychometrically. A score at or above the 75th percentile on Speilberger's measure (1988) was the most common psychometric definition. No diagnostic categories exist for anger disorders.

Second, variations in treatment integrity, clinical acumen, or experience with angry clients may also account for the variability within similar treatments.

The use of individual sessions (versus group) significantly predicted higher effect sizes on measures of non-angry positive behaviours. Individual treatment appears more effective for increasing positive behaviours and is associated with more consistent results on aggressive behaviours.

Anger treatment appears to have a more lasting effect on decreasing aggressive behaviours and increasing positive behaviours than on the subjective experience of anger (anger self-reports, physiological measures, and attitudes and cognitions) and on measures of behaviour.

HANDLE ANGER WITH SELF-HELP PACKAGE

The following self-help package of suggestions can assist us to control anger before it controls us.

- Acknowledging anger and claiming it as our own is a helpful first step. It increases self-awareness and prevents unwarranted blaming of others. Turning blame and cause into statements locates the anger where it actually is INSIDE US. We need to accept ourselves unconditionally.
- Find out what it is that triggers our anger, and then develop strategies to keep those triggers from throwing us over the edge. This shifts our anger from heart to head, from emotional level to intellectual level.
- Whenever we feel angry, we can interrogate ourselves by asking the following four questions:
  - Is this important?
  - Is my anger appropriate?
  - Is the situation modifiable?

- Is it worth taking further action?

Such an evaluation help convert our anger into a rational thought. The anger is then in our control.

- Angry people tend to demand things, and where demands are not met, their disappointments become anger. Angry people need to be made aware of their demanding nature.
- It is healthier to express our feelings in an assertive and not aggressive manner. Assertion involves taking a stand, resisting unreasonable demands, or asking for what we want. Aggression involves putting the other person down. Assertion is positive, aggression is negative. We can challenge and eliminate the anger that stands in the way of our success-without losing our assertiveness.
- Non-strenuous Yoga-like exercises, meditation, controlled breathing and relaxation imagery, can make us feel calmer. We can practise such self-help interventions daily and learn to use them automatically when we are in tense situations.
- Humour can always be relied upon to help unknot a tense situation. However, there are two cautions in using humour. First, do not try to laugh off the problems; rather use humour to help face them constructively. Second, we have to avoid harsh sarcastic humour; that is just another form of unhealthy anger expression. We can afford to frequently laugh at ourselves by directing humour against our weaknesses.
- Forgiveness involves letting go the anger and dropping the charges against the other and ourselves. Forgiving and forgetting cleans the slate and is a way of opening ourselves to future transaction. Forgiveness is a magnanimous gesture that increases personal power.

MODERN SCIENCE BEHIND AGGRESSION AND VIOLENCE

Chapter 14

Aggression works. Like all animal behaviour, aggression is the refined and tested product of more than three billion years of trial and error. So it is important to acknowledge that when discussing aggression one is addressing a suite of biologically normal, natural, adaptive behaviours.

However, aggression's evolutionary origin, biological meaning, and instrumental value provide the essential background and valuable clues to understanding all of the problematic human phenomena, which it can unfold once unleashed. Aggression, for all of its lurking threat and heart-breaking consequences, is a fact of life.

UNDERSTANDING AGGRESSION

It would seem almost trivial to define aggression, until one tries. Indeed one encyclopaedic effort identified more than 250 definitions of 'aggression'. The most common definitions equate aggression with behaviour intended to harm another.

Yet this definition fails for two important reasons. First, it assumes intent. The second failing of the "intent to harm" definition is that harm is not necessarily an outcome. Aggressive play (or human sport) may lead to minor injury, but prepares developing animals for adult success.

Throughout the animal kingdom, parents routinely act forcefully, adopt threatening postures, or physically discipline youngsters using the same motor patterns as those involved in attack and defence. Although in no way intended to condone corporal punishment (and given that physically aggressive human parents may have psychological agendas unrelated to effective child rearing), it must be noted that most human parents are compelled occasionally to administer measured, somewhat aggressive discipline; harm is the exact opposite of what is usually intended and produced.

Another problem for definition is the diversity of aggression. If aggression is regarded as a unitary concept, one needs to have a model and definition that accommodates everything from a playground stare to a nuclear war. An even more contentious issue is the proper definition of violence. More so than aggression, the term the violence implies very undesirable behaviour. It connotes

> One encyclopaedic effort identified more than 250 definitions of 'aggression'. The most common definitions equate aggression with behaviour intended to harm another.

extreme, unjustifiable aggression, usually violating social sanctions and causing destruction. Violence is virtually never attributed to non-human animals.

One popular definition stated that violence is "the threat or use of force that results, or is intended to result, in the injury or forcible restraint or intimidation of persons, or the destruction or forcible seizure of property."

However, the following proposed definition is more useful: 'Aggression is overt behaviour that involves threat or action that potentially or actually causes pain, withdrawal, or loss of resources. Violence is physically or psychologically harmful human aggression that involves the threat of using force.'

SOCIALLY ACCEPTABLE vs PROHIBITED AGGRESSION

Aggression might also be categorized according to social acceptability. Socially sanctioned aggression, depending on culture, might include rough and tumble play, spanking, contact sports, hunting, police or intelligence service actions, capital punishments, or war. Socially prohibited aggression in most cultures includes criminal assault, rape, homicide, fratricide, infanticide, child abuse, domestic violence, torture, civil disturbance, and terrorism.

These distinctions are not absolute. Spanking, infanticide of girls, and capital punishment are accepted in some cultures and considered abusive or abhorrent in others. Stoning women or men to death for perceived violation of honour codes is regarded as desirable in some places and as homicide in others. The main point is that societies reward some forms of aggression and punish others.

A closely related way to classify aggression in organized societies is to distinguish official from non-official violence. This distinction is a political-scientific one. Having formed groups adhering to social contracts that include acquiescence to authority, people often tolerate aggression in the name of collective welfare so long as recognized authorities commit the actual violence. As a general statement, even though one grows up with a clear, culture-centric picture of the distinction between permitted and prohibited aggression: 1) every society classifies aggression into its own socially acceptable and unacceptable categories, and 2) it is difficult to identify types of aggression that are universally classified as taboo.

HYPOAROUSAL vs HYPERAROUSAL-RELATED AGGRESSION

Many individuals who exhibit psychopathic traits-including non-sanctioned aggression, lack of respect for the rights of others, callousness, cruelty, lack of remorse and lack of empathy — have been found to have lower-than-usual resting heart rates and less autonomic reactivity. This has led to a classification distinguishing such Hypoarousal-related aggression from the aggression seen in anxiety disorders, mania, or stimulant intoxication, which is called Hyperarousal related.

DEMOGRAPHIC CORRELATES OF VIOLENCE

The most obvious correlate of homicide is male sex. Almost 90 per cent of those arrested for murder are men, and more than 99 per cent of serial killers are also men. Anti social personality disorder is three times as common in men, and violent suicide is also about three times as common among men as women.

Race or ethnicity is another possible factor, while poverty or lower socio-economic class is widely considered a risk factor for violent behaviour.

GENETICS AND AGGRESSION: IS IT INHERITABLE?

Commentaries on the relationship between genetics and human aggression sometimes begin with the boldfaced disclaimer, "there is no 'aggression gene'." Yet aggression is such a vital feature of human nature and variation in severity of aggression is so clearly apparent that it is very likely that one or more genes, acting alone or together — whose expression may depend on environmental factors-account for a significant proportion of the observed variance in trait aggressively.

An early study of male Swedish adoptees provided the first strong evidence that genes interact with environment to influence criminality (note that this is not equivalent to aggression). Among 862 subjects, those with neither biological nor adoptive family histories of crime had a 2.9 per cent chance of becoming criminal; those who had only criminal adoptive families had a 6.7 per cent chance; those with only biological criminal families had a 12.1 per cent chance; and those with both biological and adoptive criminal influences had an astonishing 40 per cent risk of becoming criminals. *(Craig: Bio Essays 2007)*

If biology and upbringing acted independently, one would expect about an 18.8 per cent chance of criminality for boys with both risk factors. The findings of a much higher than predicted rate, supports the theory of synergistic gene-environment interaction.

Several other adoption studies reported similar results specifically for anti-social traits. Subsequent studies identified molecular genetic traits that may interact with adverse developmental environment specifically to yield an elevated risk of adult aggression.

As expected, those who suffered maltreatment in childhood were more likely to become anti-social adults. A mutation in the gene for an enzyme Mono Amine Oxidase-A (MAOA) has been found to have a strong link to aggression.

One study reported that the protective effect of high MAOA

enzyme activity was seen among white, but not among non-white boys. Another recent study found that aggression among criminal alcoholic males was associated with the combination of higher CSF testosterone levels with the low activity MAOA variant.

Another facet of gene-environment interaction is the evidence of environment-evocative genetic-traits. For instance, an association has been reported between anti-social traits in biological parents and harsh parenting by the adoptive parents. The thought is that children bearing anti-social traits evoke harshness in the rearing parents. This may in turn provide the adverse environment in which an innate tendency to agrees will flourish.

Thus a strong case has been made out for what we have always thought — Gene Environment Interaction that is: If there is a genetic weak link, an adverse environment will bring it out.

DEVELOPMENT AND AGGRESSION

Because humans evolved to survive threatening environments in which aggressive skills were survival skills, it is readily apparent why aggression is woven into the fabric of development. The age of peak human aggression is between 2.5 years and 3.5 years. Boys are more physically aggressive than girls. Some degree of anti-social, aggressive behaviour is in fact normal in adolescent boys; the largest, the longest, the best-designed longitudinal studies, such as the Dunedin Study, have demonstrated that it is a rare boy who fails to exhibit such behaviour.

However, most people of both sexes moderate their aggression later in development, limiting conflict tactics to those generally regarded as socially sanctioned. The question addressed here is — genes aside-how non-sanctioned aggression develops. This question can be reviewed into the following domains, however, prior to embarking on this review, it is important to acknowledge a limitation:

> As expected, those who suffered maltreatment in childhood were more likely to become anti-social adults. A mutation in the gene for an enzyme Mono Amine Oxidase-A (MAOA) has been found to have a strong link to aggression.

Regrettably, the vast majority of research has been focused on boys. Their indisputably higher rates of physical aggression emerge by preschool years, and the gender gap in physical aggression increases through adolescence. A direct/indirect aggression dichotomy has been proposed in which boys' externalizing aggression is far more likely to take the form of fighting, whereas that of girls is more likely to take the form of teasing or reputation damaging.

Some evidence suggests that oppositional and aggressive girls do not usually go on to exhibit non-sanctioned physical aggression, but are at high risk of becoming anxious and depressed women. In fact, insufficient attention has been paid to studying aggression in girls and the overlap between the types of aggression in the two sexes.

PRE-AND PERI-NATAL RISK FACTORS

Among the psychosocial risk factors implicated are poverty, maternal teenage first pregnancy, single parenthood, marital discord, and low maternal intelligence quotient (IQ). Certain bio-toxicities also clearly influence the rate of subsequent aggression. Fatal exposure to alcohol increases the risk of childhood conduct disorder, although perhaps surprisingly, it remains unclear whether such exposure increases the rate of adolescent and adult violence.

In a study of children with foetal alcohol syndrome, a stable home environment reduced the risk of later anti social behaviour, suggesting an important environment-environment interaction.

Foetal exposure to maternal smoking also increases the risk of conduct disorder and adult violent criminality. Carbon monoxide and nicotine may be the responsible neurotoxins.

Nutrition is another risk factor. In one study, Dutch men whose mothers survived a wartime famine during pregnancy went on to exhibit increased rates of anti social behaviour. Foetal cocaine exposure has recently been shown to increase aggression in boys at the age of five years. Prenatal lead exposure is strongly associated with childhood aggression and less strongly with adult aggression.

Delivery complications are also a risk factor for anti social and violent behaviour. When birth complications are combined with an 'adverse' family environment-such as maternal separation or marital discord or poverty or familial criminality — the risk of violent criminality is even higher. Infants born with minor physical anomalies (e.g., low-set ears, cleft lip and palate) also have an increased risk of later criminality.

Again, when such birth anomalies are combined with problems in family life, violent offending is especially likely to occur.

POSTNATAL FACTORS: HARMFUL THING AFTER DELIVERY

Postnatal risk factors for aggression are typically divided into psychosocial versus biological, but this is a false dichotomy because: 1) a social factor such as poverty might be associated with a host of biological variables, from prenatal health care to missed vaccinations to ongoing nutritional problems to lead exposure; and 2) ultimately all psychosocial factors act by changing the brain (e.g., acute stress affects the hypothalamic pituitary axis in ways that can damage the hippocampus.)

Among the best established is the strong relationship between lead and aggressive delinquency. The major source of poisoning is deteriorating lead-based paint.

Regarding normal social factors, postnatal exposure to marital discord, single parenthood, and domestic violence all increases the risk of childhood and adolescent aggression. Many studies suggest that the likelihood of aggressive/disruptive behaviours in childhood, adolescence, and adulthood occur if children are either abused or neglected. It has been proposed that these stressors lead to aggression by somewhat different mechanisms.

Abuse may teach hyper-vigilance, a hostile attribution bias, and the use of violence to achieve goals. Neglect, in contrast, may lead to impaired emotional regulation due to deficient interactions. Statistical data link both problems to later violence. Maternal neglect or rejection in infancy, in particular, has been shown to interact with genes to elevate the risk of aggression. As mentioned earlier, the combination of genetically mediated low MAOA activity and early maltreatment is a strong predictor of adult anti-sociality.

Some studies show that early exposure to either abuse or neglect is associated with specific neurological changes, including epileptiform discharges, focal brain volume reduction, and decreased synaptic density of the hippocampus.

PEERS

By late middle childhood, roughly after the age of 10, peers loom much larger both as role models and sources of psychically salient rewards and punishments. Peer acceptance or rejection begins displacing parental feedback as a determinant of mood, and peers begin displacing parents as the source of definitive practical knowledge. This is the age at which peers begin to recognize the disturbing qualities of the aggressive subgroup and the age at which peer influences more deeply affect aggressiveness.

Two potentially vicious feedback loops can occur. First, a child, who is more aggressive may experience peer rejection, which leads to hostility and increased aggressiveness, which leads to further rejection. Second, aggressive boys will begin to find each other and associate, which reinforces their initial aggression, especially among those more prone to peer pressure. In such groups, aggressive displays become competitive and rewards accrue to the most violent surviving risk takers. In the absence of potent alternative paths of self-respect, the bad-company effect may propel otherwise moderately aggressive boys towards violence. Gangs, for some, provide an irresistible promise of affiliation, identity and warrior bonds. The negative feedback for aggression that might otherwise come from non-violent peers and parents is replaced by positive feedback for violent behaviour until, in many cases the cycle is interrupted by maturity or death.

RELATION BETWEEN TV / MEDIA AND AGGRESSION

Television viewing occupies more hours for adults in the developed world than any activity apart from work and sleep. Yet the precise effect of television watching on aggression remains disputed. A very large number of studies summarized in two meta-analyses reported that childhood television watching is associated with higher rates of aggression. However, most were very short term studies.

In perhaps the best project addressing this question, the Children in the Community Study followed children from a mean age of 5.8 years in 1976 to age 30 years in 2000. Television viewing in hours per day at the age of 14 years was strongly associated with aggressive acts against another person at the age of 16 and 22 years. Note that the content viewed was not the factor; the time spent viewing (less or more than 1 hour per day) alone predicted aggression. Thus more than the Media Content — neglect, growing up in an unsafe neighbourhood, income below poverty level, low parental education, and psychiatric disorders were all associated both with more time spent watching television and with aggression.

DOMESTIC / INTIMATE PARTNER VIOLENCE

Although it is an extremely common worldwide problem, domestic or intimate partner violence is difficult to classify. Though verbal

> Certain traits and diagnosis are associated with men who assault their intimate partners. On an average, such men are more hostile, impulsive, power oriented and tend to hold stereotyped views of gender roles. Rates of Personality Disorder, anxiety and depression are higher among spousal batterers.

and physical aggression is very common in relationships, it is unclear whether to regard this phenomenon as a unique category of aggression. It may be related to evolutionary imperatives, a disorder of attachment, personality disorder or simply that aggressive people will tend to aggress wherever they spend time. Estimates of prevalence, both major, minor aggression and sexual abuse vary from 25% to 90% !

Certain traits and diagnosis are associated with men who assault their intimate partners. On an average, such men are more hostile, impulsive , power oriented and tend to hold stereotyped views of gender roles. In some Personality studies eg: Minnesota Multiphasic Personality Inventory (MMPI), male perpetrators scored higher on the Psychopathic Deviant scale. Rates of Borderline Personality Disorder (BPD), Affective Personality Disorder (APD), anxiety and depression are higher among spousal batterers. A majority of male spouse abusers were themselves abused in childhood. Unemployment is a risk factor. Although, domestic violence is often associated with alcohol intoxication, at least 76 per cent of perpetrators have been violent when sober. Other additional risk factors include history of stalking, sexual jealousy and threatened separation. It is quite possible that men who recurrently perpetuate domestic violence may be neuro-biologically different. Research has identified five threads of evidence in this regard: 1) Autonomic

Nervous Dysregulation, 2) Low Serotonergic Function, 3) Higher Testosterone levels especially in alcoholics, 4) Abnormal threat reactivaty, and 5) History of Substance Dependence suggesting central reward deficiency is very common. But whatever the reason, domestic violence is not one homogenous neuro-psychiatric disorder but a final common pathway for multiple bio-psychological problems.

LIFE COURSES OR TRAJECTORY OF AGGRESSION

A debate exists about the typical life course or alternative trajectories of aggression. Based on the Dunedin study, it was proposed that two major patterns were distinguishable: A dangerous life-persistent pattern of aggression starting in early childhood versus a much more benign adolescent-limited pattern.

Other studies, however, suggest that there are at least three major life trajectories, two of which can be subdivided: 1a) early-childhood onset, limited duration, 1b) adolescent-onset, limited duration; 2a) early-childhood-onset, life-course-persistent, (2b) adolescent-onset, life-course-persistent; and (3) adult-onset aggression.

It is indisputable that boys' expected aggressiveness occurs in two waves: The first, during toddler years prior to gaining self-control and second, during mid to late adolescence. Thus, the most common type of aggression is type 1a, the early childhood onset, limited-duration type, given that the peak of human interpersonal aggression occurs at about age 2.5 to 3.5 years. This pattern is essentially normative.

The most common pattern of clinically referred aggression is type 1b, the adolescent-onset, limited-duration type. Adolescent aggressiveness is certainly related to hormonal factors, although several developmental theories add depth to the understanding of why adolescent boys are aggressive.

First, the role of a parent as disciplinarian shifts from control toward monitoring and the child resists that monitoring in his quest for autonomy. Second, the adolescent period forces the child to deal with increased social and cognitive demands with an incompletely developed central nervous system. Although it is very distressing and potentially dangerous, parents can be reassured that this type of aggression is common and usually time limited.

The early-onset, life persistent type, type 2a, is the best candidate for reflecting an innate and abnormal biological condition, the expression of which is perhaps triggered by environmental factors. An example might be a genetic risk factor combined with parental neglect. Those with the adolescent-onset, persistent type of aggression, type 2b, may perhaps be especially vulnerable to peer influences or to steroid hormone changes, or to share with persons with schizophrenia or other major mental disorders the poorly understood mechanism by which behavioural atypicality is not apparent until the end of development.

The least understood pattern is adult-onset aggression, type 3. A commonplace is the statement that although not all aggressive children become aggressive adults, every violent adult was an aggressive child. The occasional occurrence of the serious aggression with its first appearance in adulthood belies this claim.

One theory is that individuals who are over controlled but simmering during their development period may suddenly — and inexplicably to all appearances — explode with acts of serious adult violence. It is unknown how often such events are triggered by a psychologically meaningful provocation alone or by the co-occurrence of such a provocation with a second factor such as traumatic brain injury, covert epilepsy, substance intoxication, cerebrovascular disease, or other organic brain condition.

AGGRESSION IN CHILDHOOD

CHILDHOOD NEURO-PSYCHIATRIC DISORDERS AND AGGRESSION

Aggression is among the most common reasons for psychiatric referral of children and adolescents. Several distinct disorders frequently associated with aggression are recognized by the DSM classification system. These include Mental Retardation (MR), Autistic Disorder (AD), Pervasive Development Disorder, Attention-Deficit Hyperactivity Disorder (ADHD), Oppositional Defiant Disorder (ODD), and especially Conduct Disorder (CD).

AGGRESSION AND INTELLECTUAL DISABILITIES

The term Mental Retardation (MR) represents a basket for many undiagnosed problems. Birth hypoxia, fragile X syndrome, inborn errors of metabolism, or undetected infantile meningitis may all result in developmental delay. In 2007, the American Association on Mental Retardation changed its name to the American Association of Intellectual and Developmental Disabilities.

MR is often co-morbid with hyperactivity, impulsiveness, depression, or substance abuse. General intellectual capacity are statistically more likely to also have central nervous system problems that: 1) delay brain maturation, 2) impair the ability to learn from experience or to remember lessons, 3) impair the ability to restrain impulses, 4) deter learning complex expectations of social and legal conduct, 5) cause misinterpretation of social cues, 6) limit non-criminal opportunities for gainful employment, 7) expose individuals to situations in which others take advantage of exploiting them.

AGGRESSION AND AUTISM / ADHD /ODD

Aggression is commonly reported by parents of autistic children;

much of that aggression is hyperactivity related, consisting of self-directed injury or non-directed tantrums.

Aggression is a very common complaint of children diagnosed with Attention Deficit Hyperactive Disorder or ADHD. In fact many children diagnosed as CD in Britain are diagnosed as ADHD in America! Prevalence of ADHD in Female delinquents may be higher than in males. Lack of self-control and self-monitoring is the usual explanation in such conditions. However, frustration, low self-esteem, distress at social exclusion that these children encounter may better explain the aggression in many cases.

Oppositional Defiant Disorder (ODD) is another umbrella term weakly tethered to any consistent psychological mechanism and not shown to have any biological underpinning.

AGGRESSION AND CONDUCT DISORDER

Conduct Disorder (CD) is one of the most frequent disorders in outpatient psychiatric clinics and by far the most common diagnosis in disruptive children. The reason may be that CD is an umbrella term applied to a wide variety of behaviours of varying severity.

AGGRESSION IN ADULTS

The causes of this can vary from being an essentially normal biological behavior to a major organic / neuro-psychiatric disorder. To list a few :

INTERMITTENT EXPLOSIVE DISORDER

Intermittent Explosive Disorder (IED) involves repeated episodes of impulsive, aggressive, violent behavior or angry verbal outbursts in which you react grossly out of proportion to the situation. Road rage, domestic abuse, throwing or breaking objects, or other temper tantrums may be signs of Intermittent Explosive Disorder.

IED is the only DSM-4 disorder that explicitly requires aggression for diagnosis. Broadly it is defined as 3 such attacks in a lifetime and narrowly as 3 attacks in last 12 months.

People with IED may attack others and their possessions, causing bodily injury and property damage. They may also injure themselves during an outburst. Later, people with intermittent explosive disorder may feel remorse, regret or embarrassment.

Symptoms

Explosive eruptions, usually lasting less than 30 minutes, often result in verbal assaults, injuries and the deliberate destruction of property. These episodes may occur in clusters or be separated by weeks or months of non aggression. In between explosive outbursts, the person may be irritable, impulsive, aggressive or angry.

Aggressive episodes may be preceded or accompanied by: Irritability; increased energy; rage; racing thoughts; tingling; tremors; palpitations; chest tightness and feeling of pressure in the head. Depression, fatigue or relief may occur after the episode.

The following criteria have been proposed:

- Recurrent attacks of aggression manifested as either of the following:
    - Verbal or physical aggression towards other people, animals, or property twice weekly on an average of 1 month OR
    - Three episodes involving physical assault against other people or destruction of property over a period of one year.
- The degree of aggressiveness expressed is out of proportion to the provocation or any precipitating psychosocial stressors.
- The aggressive behavior is generally not premeditated (i.e. impulsive) and is not committed to achieve some tangible objective (e.g. power, money, intimidation etc.)
- The aggressive behavior causes either marked distress in the individual or impairment in occupational or interpersonal functioning.

- The aggressive behavior is not better accounted for by any other mental disorder.

Prognosis / Outcome

People with intermittent explosive disorder have an increased risk of:

Self-harm: They don't always direct their anger at others. They're at significantly increased risk of harming themselves, either with intentional injuries or suicide attempts. Those, who are also addicted to drugs or have another serious mental disorder, such as depression, are at greatest risk of harming themselves.

Impaired interpersonal relationships: They're often perceived by others as always being angry. This can lead to relationship problems, divorce and family stress.

Trouble at work, home or school: Other complications of intermittent explosive disorder may include job loss, school suspension, auto accidents, financial problems or trouble with the law.

PERSONALITY DISORDER

These are deeply ingrained, maladaptive patterns of behaviour; recognizable in adolescence or earlier; continuing throughout most of adult life; either the patient or others have to suffer; there is an adverse effect on the individual or society.

Symptoms

- **Affective personality disorder** –three groups:
    - Depressive personality disorder-always low in spirits; persistently gloomy view of life; brood about misfortunes; worry unduly; strong sense of duty; little capacity for enjoyment.
    - Hyperthymic personality disorder- habitually cheerful and optimistic; striking zest for living; poor judgement; periods of

irritability ,anger and even aggression when aims frustrated.

- Cyclothymic personality disorder-alternate between being low in spirits and being cheerful and optimistic; gloomy defeatist approach to life as mood changes from hyperthymic to depressive; reduced energy.

- **Anankastic personality disorder** (Obsessional personality disorder) - lack of adaptability to new situations; high moral standards; humourless approach to life; miserly; sensitivity to criticism; indecision; emotionally constricted.
- **Antisocial personality disorder** (sociopathic or asocial personality disorder) - impulsive actions; lack of guilt; failure to make loving relationships; failure to learn from adverse experiences.
- **Asthenic personality disorder** (passive or dependent personality disorder) - weak-willed; unduly complaint; lack vigour; lack self-reliance; avoid responsibility; little capacity for enjoyment.
- **Avoidant personality disorder** - hypersensitive to rejection; low self-esteem; unwillingness to enter into relationships; desire for acceptance.
- **Borderline personality disorder** – unstable relationships; undue anger; variable moods; chronic boredom; doubts about personal identity; intolerance of being left alone; self-injury; impulsive behavior that is damaging to the person.
- **Explosive personality disorder** – instability of mood with outbursts of anger and violence; no other difficulties in relationships (cf. antisocial personality disorder).
- **Histrionic personality disorder** – self- dramatization; a self-centered approach to personal relationships; a craving for excitement for novelty.
- **Narcissistic personality disorder** – grandiose sense of self-importance; preoccupation with fantasies of unlimited success, power and intellectual brilliance; attention demanding but show

little warm feeling in return; exploitive but do not give favours in return.

- **Paranoid personality disorder** – strong-sense of self-importance; suspicious; hypersensitive; cold affect; argumentative and stubborn.
- **Passive aggressive personality** – passive resistance to demands for adequate performance; stubborn; intentionally inefficient.
- **Schizoid personality disorder** – introspective; prone to engage in an inner world of fantasy rather than take action; lack of emotional warmth and rapport; self-sufficient and detached; aloof and humourless; incapable of expressing tenderness or affection; shy; often eccentric; insensitive; ill-at-ease in company.
- **Schizotypal personality disorder** – superstitious ideas; an interest in telepathy and clairvoyance; unrealistic (magical) thinking; odd forms of speech.

Prognosis / Outcome

Personality disorders tend to become rather less disorganized as the patient grows older. Patients with antisocial personality disorder over the age of 45 years comparatively present fewer problems, however, their difficulties in personal relationships tend to persist.

ANXIETY DISORDERS

These are various combinations of psychological and physical manifestations of anxiety, not attributable to real danger and occurring as a persisting state. This group in which aggression and anger are a major component includes Obsessive Compulsive Disorder.

OBSESSIVE COMPULSIVE DISORDER

Symptoms

This has two parts: (a) Obsession- recurrent persistent thoughts, impulses, phobias, or images that the patient regards as absurd and alien, while recognizing them as the product of his own mind. Initially, however, attempts are made to resist or ignore them, and (b) Compulsion – action or the need to carry out the obsessional thought. These thoughts and actions occurring repeatedly are usually dangerous, aggressive or socially embarrassing.

Prognosis / Outcome

To thirds of patients improve by the end of one year. Cases lasting beyond that run a fluctuating course, with periods of partial or complete remission lasting a few months to several years. Poor prognosis is associated with – Anankasthic personality trait, continuing stress in patient's life and severe symptoms.

AFFECTIVE DISORDERS

These are characterized by mood disturbances (inappropriate elation or depression) and usually accompanied by abnormalities in thinking and perception arising out of mood disturbances. They are of three kinds: (1) Bipolar - Recurring attacks of both mania and depression (at least one maniac / hypomaniac episode required to make this diagnosis) (2) Unipolar - recurring attack of depression only and (3) Mixed - where maniac and depressive symptoms occur simultaneously.

Symptoms

Maniac/Hypomania: A typical episode is a mood change characterized by elation with hyperactivity, over involvement in life activities, increased irritability, flight of ideas, easy distractibility and little need for sleep. All this initially attracts others but the irrationality, mood swings, aggressive behavior and grandiosity lead to marked inter-personal difficulties. The episodes begin abruptly and may last from several days to months. It is accompanied with alterations in appearance, thought, cognition and insight.

Prognosis / Outcome

In Bipolar disorder, nearly all maniac patients recover eventually. However, maniac illnesses often recur and subsequent depressive disorder is frequent. The length of remission between episodes of illness become shorter up to the thirds attack, but does not change after that. Personality is well preserved between episodes of illness. Nearly all young patients of Unipolar disorder recover, though not all elderly patients do so.

ORGANIC DISORDERS, DRUG AND SUBSTANCE ABUSE

Among the many, a few important Organic conditions are :

- Brain Tumors, Sub-dural Hematoma
- Head Injury, Epilepsy, Stroke, Drug Withdrawal
- Neurodegenerative: Alzheimer's, Parkinson's and Huntington's Diseases

Many drugs are known to give rise to aggression. To list the main ones: Alcohol, Cocaine, Amphetamines, Anabolic Steroids, Phencyclidine and Anti-Depressants (SSRI's)

TREATMENT OF AGGRESSION

The very concept of treatment of aggression gives a pause. First, majority of patients are bio-physiologically normal or at least not due to a mental disorder. Physicians are at a cross roads that many a time it is a part of human nature and many times socially sanctioned. Secondly, only a small percentage regards their behaviour as problematic and come for treatment voluntarily. Thirdly, there is a huge list of causes as enumerated above which have multi-factorial causes not many of which are apparent.

As a generalization, treatment is a combination of Psychotherapy augmented in most cases by Pharmacological medication.

GENERAL PRINCIPLES OF PHARMACOLOGICAL THERAPIES

Medications are frequently used in the management of aggression, and current psychopharmacologic treatment strategies involve treating aggression as part of each particular syndrome. Acute management focuses on calming the agitated patient, whereas chronic management aims to reduce the frequency and intensity of episodes of agitation. Long-term treatment is directed toward the underlying disorder. Additional adjunctive medications may be necessary when standard therapeutic approaches are ineffective.

Agitated patients should be offered medications as early as possible. Medication choice depends on several factors, most notably the patient's history and the assessment, even though there may be little time for a thorough assessment when an aggressive patient is a danger to him/herself or others. Medical conditions (infectious, toxic, physiologic, and metabolic causes of aggression) should be identified because they might require treatment and might affect psychopharmacologic treatment.

Benzodiazepines: is a good choice to treat acute agitation or aggression, particularly when the etiology is not clear. It is safe and effective, and is reliably absorbed when administered intramuscularly. The drug can also be administered orally, sublingually, or intravenously.

Antipsychotics: By also treating any underlying psychosis, neuroleptics can have a longer-lasting effect on agitation. Acute mania can be quickly and effectively controlled with neuroleptics, and these medications have been used to manage aggression in the elderly. However, high doses of neuroleptics can result in more adverse side effects, including akathisia (inability to sit still).

Antidepressants: Antidepressants reduce fear, irritability, and anxiety, emotions that are in the same spectrum as agitation. Current findings point to decreases in negative mood and aggressive attacks, as well as positive changes in personality traits after antidepressant treatment.

Mood Stabilizers: Mood stabilizers are primarily used for the treatment of bipolar disorder and as an adjunct treatment for schizophrenia. They are also used to treat aggression, although they are not prototypical for this purpose.

Beta Blockers: Beta-adrenergic blockers have been used to treat aggressive behaviour in a number of diagnoses, including mental retardation, autism, post traumatic brain syndromes, dementia, Huntington's disease, Wilson's disease, postencephalitic psychosis, and apparent or presumed chronic central nervous system dysfunction inferred from soft neurologic signs, abnormal electroencephalographic (EEG) findings, or clinical seizures.

GENERAL PRINCIPLES OF NON-PHARMACOLOGICAL THERAPIES

These have been around since time immemorial but have been categorized only recently. To name just a few:

- ***Insight Oriented Psychotherapy***: It is a form of treatment that helps people through understanding and expressing feelings, motivations, beliefs, fears and desires. The understanding develops in the context of a therapeutic relationship. It also strives to teach you how and why you function in the ways you do, and to clarify your motivations. It gives you self-knowledge and is useful in cases where aggression is due to depression or anxiety.
- ***Cognitive Behavior Therapy***: Cognition is the mental process of how we perceive things around us, acquire knowledge, learn, understand, remember and think at different times in our lives. Promoted by Aaron T. Beck, it is based on the theory that individuals learn to think in automatic, maladaptive ways, making irrational assumptions and holding irrational beliefs linked to painful emotions. Helping them through informed, supportive talk to reframe the problems they face in more rational, accurate, and useful ways is thought to improve their

success in dealing with life's challenges.

- ***Behaviour Modification***: Based on the work of B.F. Skinner, this technique has been developed on the theory of "Operant Conditioning". According to this every kind of behaviour is governed by reinforcing and punishing stimuli. Behaviour Modification uses a scheduled approach that rewards desired behaviour and "punishes" undesirable behaviour.
- ***Supportive Psychotherapy***: This refers to regular meetings with a sympathetic care provider. The author believes that this intervention, whether or not it occurs within the setting of another model of talk therapy, whether administrated by a mental health professional, a religious leader or another empathetic authority figure, and whether or not it is associated with medical interventions- is an essential minimum component of any therapeutic strategy.

HELP YOURSELF CONTROLLING ANGER AND AGGRESSION

If you have been diagnosed with a disorder, prevention is likely beyond your control unless you get treatment from a professional. Combined with, or as part of, treatment, these suggestions may help you prevent some incidents from getting out of control.

- ***Unlearn bad behavior***: Coping well with anger is a learned behaviour. Cognitive behavioral therapy or anger management will help you recognize what pushes your buttons and how to respond in ways that work for you instead of against you.
- ***Develop a plan***: Work with your doctor on developing a plan of action for when you feel yourself getting angry. For example, if you think you might lose control, try to remove yourself from that situation. Go for a walk or call a trusted friend to try to calm you down.

- ***Stick with your treatment***: Attend your therapy sessions, practise your coping skills, and if your doctor has prescribed medication, be sure to take it.
- ***Practice relaxation techniques***: Regular use of deep breathing, relaxing imagery or yoga may help you stay calm.
- ***Develop new ways of thinking (cognitive restructuring)***: Changing the way you think about a frustrating situation by using rational thoughts, reasonable expectations and logic may improve how you view and react to an event.
- ***Use problem-solving***: Make a plan to find a way to solve a frustrating problem. Even if you can't fix it right away, it can refocus your energy.
- ***Learn ways to improve your communication***: Listen to the message the other person is trying to share, and then think about your best response rather than saying the first thing that pops into your head.
- ***Change your environment***: When possible, leave or avoid situations that upset you. Also, scheduling personal time may enable you to better handle an upcoming stressful or frustrating situation.
- ***Avoid mood-altering substances***: Don't use alcohol or street drugs.

SEEKING PROFESSIONAL HELP

Chapter 15

"There is No Health Without Mental Health"
– This is the slogan of World Health Organization's (WHO) comprehensive Mental Health Action Plan 2013-20, adopted by the 66th World Health Assembly. Mental health includes our emotional, psychological, and social well-being. It affects how we think, feel, and act. It also helps determine how we handle stress, relate to others, and make choices. Mental health is important at every stage of life, from childhood to adolescence and through adulthood.

Over the course of your life, if you experience mental health problems, your thinking, mood, and behaviour could be affected. Positive mental health allows people to:

- Realize their full potential
- Cope with the stresses of life
- Work productively
- Make meaningful contributions to their communities
- Early warning signs

Anger in many cases is the outward expression of an underlying disorder like depression, anxiety, chronic stress etc., which may arise from a number of factors like explained earlier. However, much before they become very apparent, there are some indications. Experiencing one or more of the following feelings or behaviours can be early warning signs of the problem:

- Eating or sleeping too much or too little
- Pulling away from people and usual activities
- Having low or no energy
- Feeling numb or like nothing matters
- Having unexplained aches and pains
- Feeling helpless or hopeless
- Smoking, drinking, or using drugs more than usual
- Feeling unusually confused, forgetful, on edge, upset, worried, or scared
- Yelling or fighting with family and friends
- Experiencing severe mood swings that cause problems in relationships
- Having persistent thoughts and memories you can't get out of your head
- Hearing voices or believing things that are not true
- Thinking of harming yourself or others
- Inability to perform daily tasks like taking care of your kids or getting to work or school.

> Mental health includes our emotional, psychological, and social well-being. It affects how we think, feel, and act. It also helps determine how we handle stress, relate to others, and make choices.

It is always better to seek Professional help in early stages rather than sitting on it and hoping it will go away. Therefore, a visit to your Doctor is the First Step towards your Inner Resolve in confronting and overcoming the problem.

MEDICAL DOCTOR AND MENTAL HEALTH DISORDER / PSYCHIATRY

Psychiatry is a rich and diverse medical specialty concerned with abnormalities of the mind, namely abnormal emotions and thoughts, which may result in abnormal behaviour.

Psychiatric illness may have social, psychological and biological causes. The symptoms and signs of mental disorder are known as psychopathology. Doctors analyze a patient's psychopathology using the psychiatric history and the mental state examination. *Psychiatrists are Medical Professionals or Doctors and are registered with State Medical Council.*

Doctors use four methods of assessment: 1. Psychiatric history, 2. Mental State examination, 3. Physical examination and 4.Relevant medical, social and psychological investigation.

Information from these assessment methods is built into a differential diagnosis from which a management plan is formulated. The assessment is a holistic one which incorporates physical, social and psychological components. Similarly, treatments, for mental illness may involve physical, social and psychological treatments.

- Physical treatments may include drugs such as Antidepressants and Antipsychotics, Electroconvulsive Therapy (ECT) and, very rarely, Psycho-Surgery.
- Social treatments may involve admission in special rehabilitation settings, attendance at day hospital or day centers, some family interventions such as giving information and counseling to relatives and socio-legal advice.
- Psychological treatments may include one-to-one psychotherapy, group psychotherapy and family therapy. One-to-one psychotherapy is sometimes called inter-personal therapy. There are many different forms, such as Psychoanalysis, Cognitive Behaviour Therapy (CBT), Bio-Feedback Therapy etc.

NON- MEDICAL MENTAL HEALTH PROFESSIONALS / CLINICAL PSYCHOLOGIST

Clinical psychologists have the professional training and clinical skills to help people learn to cope more effectively with life issues and mental health problems. Psychologists help by using a variety of techniques based on the best available research and consider someone's unique values, characteristics, goals and circumstances.

Qualified Clinical Psychologists again have to be registered. In India, it is with the Rehabilitation Council of India.

Since they are not Medical doctors even if they have done Ph.D, they are not licensed to write or prescribe any drug / medication.

Practising psychologists are also trained to administer and interpret a number of tests and assessments that can help diagnose a condition or tell more about the way a person thinks, feels and behaves. These tests may evaluate intellectual skills, cognitive

> Doctors use four methods of assessment:
> 1. Psychiatric history,
> 2. Mental State examination,
> 3. Physical examination, and
> 4. Relevant medical, social and psychological investigation.

strengths and weaknesses, vocational aptitude and preference, personality characteristics and neuropsychological functioning.

Clinical psychologists can help with a range of mental health problems and use an assortment of evidence-based treatments to help people improve their lives. Most commonly, they use therapy (often referred to as psychotherapy or talk therapy). There are many different styles of therapy, but the psychologist will choose the type that best addresses the person's problem and best fits the patient's characteristics and preferences.

Therapy can be for an individual, couples, family or other group. For some conditions, therapy and medication are a treatment combination that works best. For most part psychologists work along with primary care physicians, pediatricians and psychiatrists on their overall treatment.

PREPARING FOR YOUR DOCTOR'S APPOINTMENT?

Here are the following steps that can help you make the most of your appointment:

Write down the symptoms you're experiencing, including any that may seem unrelated to the reason for which you scheduled the appointment. Keep a note of key personal information, including any major stresses or recent life changes.

Make a list of all medications, vitamins, supplements or herbal products that you're taking.

Write down questions to ask your doctor. (See Below)

Prepare a list of questions to make sure you cover everything that's important to you.

Your doctor is likely to ask you a number of questions. Be ready to answer them so you can focus on points you want to spend more time on. Your doctor may ask:

- How often do you have explosive episodes?
- What triggers your outbursts?
- Have you injured or verbally abused others?
- Have you damaged property when angry?
- Have you ever tried to hurt yourself?
- Have your outbursts negatively affected your family or work life?
- Does anything seem to make these episodes occur more often?
- Is there anything that you've found that can help calm you down?
- Has anyone else in your family ever been diagnosed with a mental illness?
- Have you suffered from a head trauma?

SOME BASIC QUESTIONS TO ASK YOUR DOCTOR:

This is a very important issue because many patients are hesitant in asking their doctor (for whatever reason) about clarifications regarding their diagnosis and treatment. Failure to do this may lead to faulty self – interpretation or worse getting wrong advice from uninformed sources. This creates an unhealthy situation right from start when unrealistic expectations arise which cannot be matched and thus starts a mutual distrust between the patient and the doctor. As mentioned earlier total trust and perseverance is the key to success.

- Why am I having these angry outbursts?
- Do I need any tests? Do these tests require any special preparation?
- Is this condition temporary or long lasting?
- What treatments are available, and which do you recommend?
- Are there any side effects from treatment?
- Are there any alternatives to the primary approach that you're suggesting?
- I have other health conditions. How can I best manage these conditions together?
- Is there a generic alternative to the medicine you're prescribing?
- How long does therapy take to work?
- Do you have any printed material on this topic? What websites do you recommend?

Don't hesitate to ask questions anytime if you don't understand something.

CONCLUSION

Chapter 16

The mere fact that you are reading this suggests that you consciously or subconsciously recognize that either anger is a major issue, which needs to be addressed or it is an evil source that is really bad for your physical, mental and spiritual health. It also interprets that this intensely negative emotion is either adversely affecting someone closer to you or denting your identity as a responsible member of the society that you are a part of.

If you agree with both the above metioned observations, then half the battle is won. This is because no philosophical or therapeutic approach can be successful without the desire and active participation of the concerned individual.

As the *Shastras* say, "*Aham Brahmasmi*" – I am the Spirit Soul, I am not this Body (Brhadaranyaka Upanishad 1.4.10 of the Yajur Veda), all this is meant for your liberation and achieving oneness with the Almighty. Your desire to conquer anger is because, at this particular moment in cosmic time and space, your *Saatvic Gunas* are high and have overcome the worldly *Rajasic* and *Tamasic* forces thus the desire to break free from their bonds.

Swami Sivananda has put the truth about anger in the right perspective. The dialogue below clearly shows how destructive anger can be and how it can be destroyed:

Anger says: "I will make the people blind and deaf. I will overpower them with wrath and suffocate them with rage. I will catch hold of even wise men. They shall neither hearken to what concerns their own happiness, nor reflect what they had read in the scriptures.

Instigated by me, Indra killed Vritra, the son of Tvashtra; Lord Siva cut off the head of Brahma; Kaushika killed the sons of Vasishtha and even the mightiest Brahmachari, Hanuman, burnt Lanka. In a moment, I can destroy even the learned, the famous, those who are attentive to duties, charitable and the mighty potentates. I can infuse fury, resentment, wrath, indignation into the minds of all in the twinkling of an eye. I am very powerful. I will disturb the *Tapas* of the aspirant and even *Yogis* and destroy serenity."

Jiva: Alas, who will help me now?

Kshama: I will. I will pull out the venomous tooth of this demon, Anger.

Visva Prema: I will. And I am the water to quench the fire of anger.

> Anger says, "I will make the people blind and deaf. I will catch hold of even wise men. They shall neither hearken to what concerns their own happiness, nor reflect what they had read in the scriptures."

Viveka: I will. When I rise, anger dies.

So, there are three elements to control anger: 1) *Kshama* or patience and forgiveness; 2) *Visva Prema* or Universal love towards all; and 3) *Viveka* or the intellectual ability to discriminate between the real and the unreal or the right and the wrong.

As your Soul is Supreme and it wants to identify with the Almighty, you have to unleash its power yourself.

SELF HELP tools and techniques to control and eradicate anger:

- Be alert. Pray. Do more meditation. Practise Introspection or Self Enquiry. Keep a watch over your mind. Listen to soothing music in a fragrant atmosphere. It will activate and awaken your *Nadi* as well as your *Chakras*.
- See God in all. Submit to God's will. Then you cannot get angry. Think about the harmful consequences that your anger will create – anger will go away.
- Make it a rule to get up early every morning to review in your mind all the occasions you may encounter in the course of the day, both favourable and unfavourable, and visualize the passions they may provoke. Then, prepare in yourself beforehand how to control them at the very beginning, without allowing them to develop, so that you will never be taken unawares by any moment of passion, but will always be ready to resist them, without being troubled with anger or enticed by lust.
- In the morning, meditate on the virtue of patience. Manifest

it during the day. Take a vow, 'I will practise endurance and forgiveness during the day'. Speak sweetly. Bear insult and injury with fortitude and understanding.

- Keep congenial company. Go for spiritual talks as often as possible. Read spiritual books for at least 15 minutes a day.
- Remember and read about the lives of saints. Derive inspiration from them. You will develop love and forgiveness.
- Give up intoxicating liquors, meat and tobacco.
- Always remember the teachings of various religions and philosophies (*Shastras*) narrated above and practise the Anger Management teachings they offer.
- If you find it difficult to control anger, leave the place at once. Take a long walk. Drink cold water. Meditate any peace mantra or count from 1 to 30. Anger will subside.
- Stand as a witness of the *Vritti* of anger. Be indifferent to it. Do not identify yourself with it. Identify yourself with the *Atman* or the Soul. Fill the mind with ideas of love, joy, etc.
- Develop patience to a considerable extent. People lose their temper when they become impatient. Allow the mind to dwell constantly on the opposite of anger, the virtue of patience. This is the *Pratipaksha Bhavana,* method of *Raja Yogins*.
- Do not give vent to anger. Control the body first. Have physical control. Practise this again and again. Be regular in your meditation. This will give you great inner spiritual strength.
- Food has a great deal to do with irritability. Take *Saatvic* diet, which includes milk, fruits, *moong-ki-dal,* curd, spinach, barley, groundnuts and butter milk. Stay away from hot spices and *Rajasic/Tamasic* foods.
- Observe silence for two hours daily. Occasionally, observe it for the whole day. This will put a check on the impulse of speech. When a man gets excited, he speaks anything and everything. He has no control over the organ of speech.
- *Prana* entwines the mind like a creeper. *Pranayama* leads to the

> A physically healthy body is the first pre-requisite for starting any method for anger control. Lord Buddha puts it, "To keep the Body in good health is a duty, otherwise we shall not be able to keep our mind strong and clear."

control of mind. *Pranayama* will put a break on the impulse of speech. It will give you abundant energy to check anger.

- Do not use abusive words. Become a man of measured words. If a man abuses or insults you, keep quiet. Identify yourself with *Atman. Atman* is the same in all. It can never be hurt or insulted.
- An enlightened person denies the body and mind as illusory sheaths. He does Self Enquiry on 'Who am I' and practises '*Neti-neti*' or Via Negativa, which means "not this, not this", or "neither this, nor that" That is to understand the nature of *Brahman* by first understanding what is not *Brahman*.
- If you entertain passion or bad thoughts just look into the defects of anger and the benefits of patience, you will never become angry.
- Find the real cause of anger and try to eradicate it. Do not identify with it. The combined method of all that is meditation, introspection, *pranayama* and *asanas* is more effective.
- Ask yourself this question: "Will the object of my anger matter ten years from now?" Chances are that you will see things from a calmer perspective.

WHEN DO YOU REQUIRE PROFESSIONAL ASSISTANCE?

This is perhaps the most difficult question to answer since only you can define the problem and also find the way to solve it. All the philosophies and therapies are but a means to the end. However as said before – better sooner than later. As discussed earlier, there are various severities of anger, ranging from irritability to violence associated aggression, substance abuse, physical diseases and mental disorders causing anger or related behaviour.

Anger in true sense, according to many mental health experts, does not just happen in isolation. In many cases, it is associated with other mental conditions like stress, depression, anxiety, etc. In fact, it can be an outward response to them which expresses itself as anger or aggression. For example, a hot pan is not hot in itself but the underlying fire makes it so, thus, putting water on such a pan might cool it for a short time, but till the fire below is not extinguished, it will continue to become hot.

A physically healthy body is the first pre-requisite for starting any method for anger control. Beautiful flowers do not grow on rotting plants and as Lord Buddha puts it, "To keep the Body in good health is a duty, otherwise we shall not be able to keep our mind strong and clear." So, as you normally get your car checked up before a journey, get a complete physical examination done and get treated for any ailments. Be sure to inform your doctor of all the medications you are taking, as many drugs have side-effects.

Another reason for taking a medical opinion is that since Yoga *Asanas* are an integral part of achieving both physical and mental health, certain diseases do not allow you to perform a few *Asanas*.

The following conditions require that you take professional assistance:

- When anger disrupts your daily personal or professional life and disturbs positive relationship with family and friends. Anger tends to disrupt both. Assess through your ANGER-O-METER.
- When unexpressed anger is the dominant thought in your mind.
- When anger is associated with violence – Aggression, IED.
- When anger is associated with drugs, alcohol or substance abuse.
- When anger or aggression is associated with Adult Neuro-

Find the real cause of anger and try to eradicate it. Do not identify with it. The combined method of all that is meditation, introspection, *pranayama* and *asanas* is more effective.

psychiatric disorder, e.g., Schizophrenia, Head Injury, Stroke, Tumours, Neuro-degenerative disorder, like Parkinsonism, Alzheimer's, Epilepsy, etc.

- When anger or aggression is associated with Childhood Neuro-psychiatric disorders, e.g., Mental retardation, Autism, ADHD, CD, etc.
- Lastly, whenever you are in doubt: there are times when you need to know your progress even when you are using Self–Help techniques, simply share your problems and thoughts with a sympathetic trained person, which you may not be able to do with family or friends.

Total Health Foundation, is a Charitable Society formed in July 2005 and formally registered under The Societies Registration Act 1860, four years ago. Its members consist of eminent doctors, lawyers, policymakers, social activists, educationists and corporate leaders, hailing from across the globe. The Foundation is truly International and aims to extend its objectives beyond geographical boundaries. The Society also aims to provide expert healthcare assistance and advice both in person and online. Helpline and Telemedicine services for mothers and children, senior citizens, women, destitute are our key agenda. The Foundation is under the process of collaborating with the government in implementing various National Health Care Programs and has already conducted numerous Free Health Camps apart from providing financial aid to destitute children. Additionally, the Foundation is opening Charitable Outpatient Clinics; and has tied up with many expert doctors from the US and UK who visit India every year to provide Free medical advise to many patients.

For further details, log on to www.drpsbawa.com or email to drpsbawa@gmail.com.